Jean de la Guérivière

Translated from the French
by Florence Brutton

# The Exploration of Africa

Overlook Duckworth
Woodstock · New York · London

# Contents

# I

# These white men who came from the sea

The Ancients, who thought the Earth was flat, never conceived the existence of America or Australia. But they sensed the immensity of sub-Saharan Africa, out beyond the fortified boundary — the limites — built by the Romans on the borders of the Sahara. The barriers to exploration were the desert and the trade winds, which blow obliquely across the Atlantic Ocean, condemning any early sailing ship to a one-way trip south. Not even a galley with oars could make the journey back. Cape Juby, at the extreme southern tip of Morocco, was the limit of ancient navigation; no captain who went beyond that point ever returned to tell the tale.

# Deepest, darkest Africa remained shrouded in mystery

**The only Africans known to the Greeks and** Romans were the Nubians, from the north of present-day Sudan, who had been trading with the Egyptians since early times.

Unaffected by the trade winds, the Ancients sailed across the Mediterranean to Egypt and reached the shores of Eritrea—the coastal region to the north of present-day Ethiopia—several centuries before Christ. The Roman historian Sallust (Gaius Sallustius Crispus), governor of Africa Nova, or Nubia, in 46 B.C. referred in his writings to "Negroes" but these were in fact Ethiopians. Deepest, darkest Africa remained shrouded in mystery; no merchant, soldier, or sailor really knew what lay beyond the sands of the Sahara. Early geographers filled the empty spaces on their maps with fantastic imaginary animals, a habit that persisted until the 15th century, when these were replaced by more realistic renderings of fauna, accompanied by the words *"Hic sunt leones"* (Here are lions). Until that time, Ptolemy of Alexandria's *Geography*, written in Arabic circa 160 A.D., was the standard geographic reference. The book shows just how little was known at the time about Africa beyond 950 miles south of Gibraltar. In the 1400s, a merchant brought the book from Constantinople to Florence, where it was translated into Latin in 1409 as a gift for Pope Alexander V. The *Geography* was one of the first works to be printed on a Gutenberg press. Once accessible in a language spoken by the European elite, it became the late-medieval standard reference work on Africa. Yet the rendering of the western sub-Saharan coastline and interior in the *Geography* is pure fabrication. It features places that bear no resemblance to any known land, among them "Libia interior" and "Ethiopa sub Egipto," the latter ascribed as the home to "white elephants, rhinoceroses, and tigers." Elsewhere we find more honest references to *terra incognita*.

## Ibn Battuta, envoy of Islam

Europeans, who were under the influence of Ptolemy, didn't know that one man had already been to sub-Saharan Africa and could actually speak about it. Ibn Battuta, a Muslim born in Tangiers in 1304, acquired a taste for travel while on pilgrimage to Mecca in 1327. In the fifteen years it took to return to his native Morocco, he had visited a large part of North Africa and Asia. In 1352, the Sultan of Morocco sent Battuta on a reconnaissance trip that would last several months and take him all the way to Gao, in the sub-Saharan kingdom of Mali. Gao was the chief destination of the Berber caravans that crossed the Sahara in search of gold nuggets from the basins of the upper Niger and upper Senegal. Payment was made in the form of fabrics, metal, weapons, and horses that the Berbers brought with them. But in addition to worldly goods, Arab traders also brought the Islamic faith, and it was this aspect of sub-Saharan culture that most interested the Moroccan Sultan. Throughout the world of Islam, Ibn Battuta's account of his travels became famous, as much for its observations of Islamic life as for its geographical content. The record that he dictated to his secretary at the end of the trip is titled *The Rihla of Ibn Battuta*, "rihla" being the word for the log books of Arab merchants. But Ibn Battuta's book is much more than a conventional *rihla*. Despite its errors, it stands as the very first reasonably accurate eyewitness account of Africa.

*When they reached the Indian Ocean, the Portuguese encountered a different kind of ship designed for wind patterns unlike those on the Atlantic. The Muslims were masters of the seas and had long dominated the spice and slave trades.*

**Opposite**
The magnificent caravels captivated the imagination of European writers and artists for many years. Sailings to the Indies via Africa inspired *The Lusiades*, published by Camoens in 1572 and regarded as a formative masterpiece of Portuguese literature.

An author more widely read in Europe than Ibn Battuta was Al-Hassan ibn Muhammad al-Fasi (born in Granada circa 1483, died in Tunis, 1555), known as Leo the African. This intrepid explorer had the advantage of speaking a language that Europeans could understand, and he shared their ways of thinking. While teaching Arabic in Rome, he converted to Catholicism, and in 1550 he published a book in Italian called *A Description of Africa*. It is mainly an account of his travels on foot through what we now know as Egypt and the Sudan. The writer makes a clear distinction between the lands of "Barbary," Numidia, and Libya, and "The Land of the Blacks." What struck him most were the giraffes with "heads like camels and ears like oxen" and the crocodiles that "ate fish, land animals, and men."

## "Sons of the water"

Who were the first Christians to set foot on the sub-Saharan continent? Several countries compete for the honor, among them the French, who for many years claimed that "sailors from Dieppe" (in Normandy) landed in present-day Ghana in the early 1400s. In 1402, another Norman, Jean de Béthencourt, set sail from La Rochelle to conquer the Canary Islands. Béthencourt's expedition is documented, but there is no evidence to support the story of the French landing in Ghana. No written records from native sources survive; African folklore is all that remains to impart the culture shock experienced by these people, who had no concept of long-distance travel, upon seeing white men emerge from the sea. This was the time of the "silent commerce" that long preceded the great explorations—a time aptly described by Amadou Hampâté Bâ of Mali, one of the great French-speaking African writers of our time; for the coastal populations, these early European explorers were the "sons of the water."

## The Portuguese pioneers

In Portuguese, the verb *explorar* means to explore, to exploit, and to do business. All three meanings apply to Prince Henry the Navigator (1394-1460), the man who brought the age of exploration to African shores and thereby turned his small country into a world power. After playing a part in the capture of Ceuta, in Morocco, in 1417, Henry was determined to convert the black population of the southern Sahara to Christianity. He was also looking for a way into that "land of gold" in western Africa, much talked about by Arab traders along the trans-Saharan routes. To help him in his task, Henry had a new asset: the caravel, a small-scale sailing vessel with numerous advantages, including

TRADEING ON Yᵉ COAST OF AFRICA  THE SOUTHWELL FRIGATE  TRADEING ON Yᵉ COAST OF AFRICA

Prior to the era of great explorations came the period of
"silent commerce," during which Europeans would arrive on
African shores and lay out their wares on the beach, light a big fire, and return
to their boats. The Africans, seeing the smoke, would emerge
from the forests, take the objects left by the Europeans and deposit
riches of their own in exchange.

We know of this period through the local
legends that circulated among the coastal populations, who believed
that the Europeans were the "sons of the water,"
served by the spirits of the oceans....

Amadou Hampâté Bâ, *Oui mon commandant!*

*Europe found a gateway to the Indian Ocean by advancing in steps down the* African coastline.

a rudder for easy steering and a form of sailing rig that combined the benefits of the triangular (lateen) sails of the Mediterranean vessels with the square sails used on Nordic ships.

These new developments meant that sailing vessels were no longer entirely at the mercy of prevailing winds. Gradually, Prince Henry's sailors pushed farther and farther south. In 1434, Gil Eannes rounded Cape Bojador off the coast of present-day Western Sahara; in 1444, Dinis Diaz discovered Cape Verde off the coast of present-day Senegal. By the time Henry died, the Portuguese had already reached Sierra Leone, and soon thereafter the days of "silent commerce" were over. From this time on, the Africans were forced to paddle out in their pirogues to meet the "sons of the water," who, because of their rudders, were now forced to drop anchor some distance from shore. As a Portuguese historian puts it, it was a time of "caravels versus caravans," and the caravels were the eventual winners. Ships from the banks of the Tagus were already supplying the Africans with goods that were both more attractive and less expensive than the imported craftwork that arrived by camel. Spirits, mirrors, and manufactured pearls proved more popular than handmade leather and copper items.

Henry's nephew John II, "The Perfect," King of Portugal from 1481 to 1495, shared his uncle's interest in Africa and its treasures. With the Pope's agreement, John assumed the title "Lord of Guinea" and commissioned the building of São Jorge da Mina (Saint George of the Mine) on the coast of the future Ghana. It was the first trading post on the African Gold Coast. John then gave Bartolomeu Diaz command of a mission to sail to the Indies by way of Africa. On board his two caravels were six Africans dressed in European clothes, who were to be dropped off at various points along the coast. Their orders were to liaison with the natives, showing them the commodities – gold, spices and ivory – the Portuguese wanted. When the last African had disembarked, the two caravels were caught in a storm and blown out to sea for thirteen days, during which Diaz had unwittingly rounded the southern tip of Africa, which he would later name the Cape of Storms and John II would rename the Cape of Good Hope. On 3 February 1488, the caravels dropped anchor roughly 250 miles from the site that would later become Cape Town. Here Diaz put up a *padrao*, a huge stone marker topped by a cross, which marked the Portuguese territorial claim. He then continued along the east coast of Africa for a few more days, in completely uncharted territory, before his men took fright and forced the ship to turn back. Diaz returned to Portugal in December 1488, after rounding the dreaded Cape in the opposite direction.

## Spices and Christians

Ten years later it was Vasco da Gama's turn to visit the Indies. Christopher Columbus had discovered the New World by accident in 1492, while looking for a new route to the Indies. Da Gama, by contrast, knew exactly which way to go: along the coast of Africa. Three new ships were custom-built for the expedition. Among the passengers were priests, a sailor who spoke Arabic, and a Congolese native to act as interpreter. The ships also carried a dozen

**Above**
Vasco de Gama, appointed Viceroy of the Indies in 1524 and founder of Portugal's first bases in Mozambique. After exploring the coasts of Africa, the Lisbon sailors were destined for more adventures in India, home of such exotic-sounding places as Cochin, Calicut, and Goa.

criminals under sentence of death, to be used as messengers or hostages, or to be bartered for goods. The route extended through the Gulf of Guinea, the Cape of Good Hope, and Zanzibar. When they reached the Indian Ocean, the Portuguese encountered ships of a completely different type — large, ocean-going dhows built by the Muslims and designed for wind patterns unlike those on the Atlantic. Muslim sailors were the masters of the seas and had long dominated the spice and slave trades. It is not hard to imagine the atmosphere of mistrust when Christian and Muslim met.

## The "Amazons" of Monomotapa

Another short-lived Portuguese trust territory was the exotic-sounding "kingdom" of Monomotapa, which lies on the borders of present-day Zimbabwe and Mozambique. Several tribal chiefs were competing for the title of "emperor" of Monomotapa, and the Portuguese, who had established a base on the Zambezi River, intervened in favor of the main contender. In 1607, in exchange for their support, the Portuguese were granted a monopoly of the gold mines in the region. Although they never actually mined in earnest, they did maintain a small garrison at the "court" of the monarch until 1759. The adventures of

the Lisbon sailors in Monomotapa caught the popular imagination and even inspired a book by the then-famous Italian explorer and historian Filippo Pigafetta (not to be confused with François-Antoine Francesco-Antonio Pigafetta, another travel writer to whom he was related). The book, based on the first-hand account of one of the Portuguese explorers, and published in 1591, marks the first reference to African "Amazons." This fantasy would re-emerge many years later, when the French conquered Dahomey (later Benin, now part of Nigeria, in Western Africa).

## Olfert Dapper and the "Land of the Negroes"

In 1668, Olfert Dapper, a Lutheran Dutchman who had never set foot outside Holland, wrote a book entitled *Description of Benin*. It was published in Amsterdam by the engraver Jacob Van Meurs and featured some particularly fine etchings of the Congo, although the descriptions of the region in the text itself are only marginally noteworthy. The book is based entirely on contemporary sources, and what was more interesting, on interviews with returning travelers. By the late 17th century, the Dutch East India Company was gradually ousting the Portuguese from West Africa, so Dapper found no shortage of people to interview. What's more,

**Above, left**
Thanks to the enterprising spirit of its explorers, Portugal was the first European country to acquire African colonies; it was, however, the last to give them up.

**Above, right**
Henry the Navigator, driven by a combination of evangelizing and entrepreneurial zeal, turned the town of Sagres, in the Algarve, into an immense dockyard.

Guerrier du Congo.

Roi de Loango.

Dansseuse de Loango.

Femme de Loango.

perhaps because he was a scholar and a humanist, his account of their experiences reveals a degree of openmindedness that was rare at the time.

Still, much of the book is sheer fantasy and it conflicts substantially with what is now known to be true. For example, the chapter on the "Land of the Negroes" features a description of a fabulous animal that "many people believed was descended from a man and a monkey." The author continues: "There is no mistaking its appearance. This is without a doubt the famous satyr of ancient times, frequently spoken of by Pliny the Elder and the Roman poets, based on hearsay and untrustworthy accounts."

On the subject of lions, Dapper wrote that "the shameful parts of a woman's body are so repellent to this animal that it flees on sight." The book had all the right ingredients to become a cult phenomenon with Africa specialists, and the author himself now has a foundation and a museum of African art named after him: the Dapper Foundation in Amsterdam and the Musée Dapper in Paris.

Olfert Dapper was the first person whose interest in Africa extended beyond its geography to include its people as well. His descriptions of ethnic societies make no value judgments and display little of that intrinsic superiority expressed by European writers of the time toward non-Christian cultures. The result is a complex picture of African life based on what we would now call an "interdisciplinary" approach. For example, he refers to "cults" rather than "superstitions" when describing African religions. At a time when other Europeans were busy

**Opposite**
18th-century engravings.

**Far left**
Early 17th-century Beninese bronze plaque displaying a rigorously objective impression of a Portuguese soldier. Bronze bas-relief carvings marked the Golden Age of art in Benin.

**Opposite**
Head of a black woman, from the same period of Beninese art. Masks had religious meaning for animist cultures, but this sculpture was "art for art's sake."

*The Kingdom of Benin was in its* Golden Age
*and producing some of the most spectacular*
*art ever to come out of Africa*

discovering "savages," Dapper shows an aesthetic interest in a variety of African objects. Of course, nobody knew then that the Kingdom of Benin was in its Golden Age, and producing some of the most spectacular art ever to come out of Africa.

## Curiosity cabinets

The late 1400s saw an efflorescence of Afro-Portuguese art based on European designs executed by African craftsmen. Sculpted hunting horns, crucifixes, and ornately carved cutlery graced every royal table, and African curios were much in demand. Canvasses by the Dutch masters reveal that even rich, enlightened burghers were not averse to displaying an African weapon or two on their walls. Meanwhile, travelers returned with their bags full of African mementos: flora and fauna (shells, butterflies, dried leaves) and native artifacts. The Dutch were the first to design "curiosity cabinets" for their collections, and

the rest of Europe soon followed. Ivory and rhinoceros horns were also used by European artists in their own designs.

Europeans were increasingly curious about the "Black Continent" and Dapper's *Description of Benin* was soon available in all the major European languages; the French edition of 1686 was followed by English and German editions in 1670. They were all printed from the original copper plates made by Jacob Van Meurs, then sold by his widow to a group of publishers in Amsterdam. The Portuguese were no longer the only ones with a taste for African exploration and an interest in the African coastline. By the latter half of the 17th century, the English had established settlements all over the Gulf of Guinea; the French, after founding Saint-Louis, in Senegal, in 1658, settled in Dahomey in 1671, and then on the Ivory Coast a few years later.

## Gold in exchange for wigs

Dapper claimed that his book was mainly intended as a source of advice for merchants interested in trading with Africa. Given that there was no African currency at the time (if we exclude shells used by the natives), early trade was based exclusively on barter. This gave rise to a thriving little European industry dedicated to providing the Africans with exactly what they wanted; in addition to cottons and silks, they were especially fond of old clothes, cocked hats, and even wigs. Cheap jewelry and trinkets also went down well: pipes, mirrors, padlocks, bells, fake pearls, glass beads, and other items still commonly found in children's cereal boxes. The

**Above**
17th-century English cutlery with carved ivory handles. (There was once a time when African ivory graced every grand European table. Rhino horn was also used to make cutlery.

**Above**
Carved ivory bracelets from Benin.

**Opposite**
Although Portuguese navigation extended farther and farther down the African coastline throughout the 15th century, their maps were deliberately imprecise: there could be no question of giving away any secrets to the English or French. Indeed, in 1504 Portuguese cartographers were forbidden to extend the coastline beyond São Tomé e Principe. It is not surprising, therefore, that Dutch maps from Amsterdam, which often included instructions in several languages, soon became more popular.

most expensive goods — long, elaborately decorated rifles — were reserved for local chieftains, usually known ironically as "kings" or "dukes." In exchange, the Africans supplied the European crews with staple foods (millet, fish, poultry), gum Arabic (exuded by tropical acacia trees), melegueta pepper or grains of Paradise (*Afromomum melegueta*, also known as Guinea pepper), ostrich feathers, and especially ivory and gold. During the early 1700s, European foundries cast nearly two tons of bullion a year from gold dust supplied by countries in the Gulf of Guinea. The precious dust was measured using weights in various metals, these days much sought after by collectors. Because the Africans were suspected of fixing the scales, white brokers were always in charge of the weighing procedure. In addition to knowing about gold dust, a good broker could also tell a fake gold nugget from the real thing.

## Coastal garrisons

So far, African exploration had remained largely maritime, mainly because the endless African coastline was largely impenetrable. The rivers were huge and fast-flowing—not the kind of waterways on which the Europeans were keen to venture. There were few charted estuaries, much to the dismay of the European cartographers who plotted the sailing guides known as *portolanos*. These often beautifully illuminated and embellished charts originally covered only the Mediterranean Basin, but from the 15th century they began to include Africa as well.

From the middle of the 16th century, more advanced printing methods made it possible to produce cheaper maps, and cartography became a major business in Amsterdam. Maps of continental Africa, however, remained as imprecise as ever.

What the navigators needed to know was the location of the forts built by the Portuguese along the coast from the Atlantic to the Indian Ocean. The 16th-century Portuguese colonialists, following in the footsteps of their predecessors, who had marked their passage with *padraos*, built fortified trading posts on carefully selected sites. Some of these garrisons were later captured by the English and French, but others remain standing today. With evocative names such as Fort Jesus (Mombasa) and São Jorge da Mina (Ghana), they make the itinerary of a trip along the African coast sound like a Catholic pilgrimage.

Islands also changed ownership — and names — in the course of history. Mauritius, for example, was first discovered by the Portuguese in 1505, then settled by the Dutch until 1710, taken by the

*From the middle of the next century* **more advanced printing methods** *made it possible to produce cheaper maps, and cartography became a major business in Amsterdam.*

French in 1715 (who called it L'Ile de France), and finally by the English in 1810. St. Helena, Napoleon's island of exile 3,200 miles off the coast of Angola, has a similar history; it was discovered by the Portuguese on 21 May 1502, then settled by the Dutch and again annexed by the British around 1658. São Tomé e Principe and the Cape Verde Islands, on the other hand, remained consistently under Portuguese rule from the 15th century to the proclamation of independence in 1975. "Desert islands" (not all of which were deserted) are a feature of early accounts by navigators and were in many cases discovered before the African coastline itself.

**A black "prince" at the court of the Sun King**

In 1698, two Frenchmen returning from the maritime kingdom of Assini (on the Ivory Coast) presented to Louis XIV a so-called "prince" named Aniaba. They claimed he had been given away by his father as a token of admiration for the Sun King, but it was whispered that he had simply been bought as a servant. Whatever the case, Aniaba became a great favorite at court. Initially a mere curiosity of the court (like Montesquieu's Persians or Goldsmith's Chinese, an intrepid traveler who views the culture in ways surprising to the natives), he was instructed in the Catholic religion by Bishop Jacques Bossuet and baptized at the Church of Saint-Sulpice in Paris. Then, with none other than Louis XIV as a godfather, Aniba embarked on a new career as captain of the royal cavalry. However, in spite of the handsome allowance he received from his noble godfather, Aniaba soon ran into debt. It was clearly time for him to

return home—which he did in 1701, having decided, with no false modesty, to rename himself Hannibal. He ended his days as a local chieftain on the borders of Togo Land, a far cry from the court of the Sun King, where he had been long forgotten by his former admirers.

**Botanical collections**

Africa had become a fashionable subject in European governing and intellectual circles. Extending beyond the taste for "spices," a growing and more serious interest in the exotic African flora and fauna began to take hold. In 1726 France passed a law summoning ships' masters

**Above**
Two Dutch navigators sitting astride a giant tortoise on the island of Mauritius. Animals and birds on remote desert islands were completely tame when they first met humans. But things soon changed as man's hunting instinct got the better of him.

*The seductive Aniaba was **instructed** in the Catholic religion by **by Bishop Jacques Bossue**, then baptized at the Church of Saint-Sulpice in Paris. **His godfather was none other than Louis XIV himself.***

DOM MATHEO-LOPES. Ambassadeur...

from Nantes (a port in western France) to "return with specimens of seeds and plants found in the different places they landed." They were to deliver these specimens to their local apothecaries, who in turn were to "send to the Royal Garden of Medicinal Herbs, [the Jardin des Plantes in Paris] any specimens it might not already possess." The Jardin des Plantes (now part of the National Museum of Natural History) was opened to the public in 1640, and in 1739 the French naturalist Georges-Louis Leclerc De Buffon (c. 1725-1773) was appointed director. Buffon, internationally famous for his *Histoire naturelle, générale et particulière*, was a member of several European academies and corresponded with many of the most prominent scientists of the Enlightenment. One of them was the Scots aristocrat James Bruce, Laird of Kinnaird (1730-1794), who would discover the source of the Blue Nile. Bruce was also one of a new breed of explorer who went to Africa not for purposes of material gain but to unravel the secrets of the "Dark Continent." In the

1770s, following in the footsteps of a handful of earlier European explorers, Bruce set out for darkest Abyssinia (present-day Ethiopia). He then suffered an accident at sea, when bags containing vital instruments and drawings were lost overboard and he very nearly drowned. At that point, Bruce was about to abandon the mission, but Buffon interceded, persuading Louis XV to send out fresh supplies and equipment, thus allowing Bruce to continue his research. Such outstanding examples of European cooperation are far from common in the history of exploration.

Michel Adanson (1727-1806) was another preeminent French naturalist of the Enlightenment. Like Buffon, Adanson also knew a Scot: the banker John Law, who in 1719 founded the Compagnie de l'Occident et des Indes. The directors of this company were men of an inquiring mind, thirsty for new products with good business potential: rubber, coffee, tea, pepper, indigo, and quinine. In 1849, with business in Louisiana and Asia not booming as it had been, the company looked for new markets, especially in Africa. Adanson was commissioned to investigate commercial planting opportunities in Senegal, ultimately growing cotton and indigo in the gardens of Fort Saint-Louis. In the course

**Right**
African oil palm.

Elaeis guineensis L.

I have to admit that, to judge from its shape alone,

the monkey species could be mistaken for a variety of

the human species. This is because the Creator

gave much the same shape to both the animal and the human body;

man's shape, like that of all animals, forms part of

His grand design. However, while He gave man a

monkey-like appearance, He also filled his animal body with

His divine breath. Had he granted the same privilege to an

altogether lowlier creature, not the monkey but a base and,

to our eyes, hopelessly clumsy creature, then that species would soon

have become man's rival. Thanks to its quickened spirit, it would

have thought, talked, and triumphed over all other species. That is why,

whatever the resemblance between the Hottentot and the monkey,

the difference between them is huge. Because man's

inner self is filled with thought and his outer self is expressed by speech.

Buffon, *Histoire naturelle*, late 18th century

A LEIDE, Chez PIERRE VANDER AA.

of his travels, he also collected specimens of plants and stones, either picking them up along the way or buying them from Arab traders from the interior. On his return to France six years later, he handed his collection over to Buffon for the Jardin des Plantes, and in 1757 he published *Histoire naturelle du Sénégal*, hailed as the first book on the African flora. At about the same time, the Swedish botanist Carl von Linné (1707-1778) founded the binomial system of biological nomenclature that names plants and animals by means of two Latin names: the first (with initial capital) indicates the genus to which the organism belongs and the second indicates the species. Linné is better known as Carolus Linnaeus, because his major works are in Latin, the lingua franca of the European scientific community of the time. His system led to the classification of a wide variety of African species.

## A menagerie at the Jardin des Plantes

In 1793, the Jardin des Plantes also opened a zoo. One of its first residents, previously kept in an annex of the Château de Versailles, was a South African mammal, related to the zebra and the horse, called a quagga. Shortly afterward, however, the sad death of a captive lion prompted the celebrated French naturalist Etienne de Lacépède (1756-1825) to make a plea for an end to caged animals. "Images of imprisonment and slavery should be kept out of the sight of a liberated people" he wrote in a letter to "those public establishments known as menageries." The view he expressed was in keeping with the spirit of the French Revolution, and it also heralded the modern concepts of humane treatment of animals. In 1798, the French Republican army made a triumphal entry into Paris with a collection of wild animals confiscated from the Stadtholder (head of state) of Holland, William V, Prince of Orange (1748-1806). The public was instantly seduced by a pair of elephants named Hanz and Parkie, described as lovers by the press. But the biggest attraction was the monkeys, because of their uncanny resemblance to humans.

## Diderot's Encyclopedists and the first missionaries

The *Encyclopédie ou Dictionnaire raisonné des sciences, des arts et des métiers, par une Société de Gens de lettres* was

published under the direction of the French philosopher Denis Diderot in 1751. It contains a wealth of material by a group of French philosophers—including d'Alembert, Rousseau, and Voltaire—and gives expression to many of the most important intellectual and social developments of its time. However, in spite of the information provided by prominent naturalists, the book nevertheless reveals just how little was known about sub-Saharan Africa at the time. The entry on "Afrique" is restricted to just fifty lines and informs the reader in the second paragraph that "Trade is confined to the coast since the regions inland remain undiscovered." The striking display of ignorance in the chapter on Negroes ("Nègre," volume XI) elicits dismay from the modern reader. What, for instance, is to be made of the paragraph on "white Negroes," (commonly known as albinos), which reads as follows: "There were those who thought that white Negroes were the fruit of monstrous commerce between the big monkeys and the Negresses. Whatever the case, it seems that we do not know all the varieties and vagaries of nature; it maybe that the African interior,

about which Europeans know so little, is home to large numbers of peoples of an entirely unknown species."

Strange as it may seem, some of the writings by freethinking scholars, such as the contributors to the *Encyclopédie*, are based on the accounts of religious orders. For example, the chapter on Negroes in Buffon's *Histoire naturelle, générale et particulière* (see above) quotes the Jesuit missionary and writer Father Pierre de Charlevoix. However short-lived, Portuguese evangelical zeal in the Kingdom of the Congo had not been in vain. Dominicans and Jesuits followed in their paths, establishing two French missions in Senegal, on Gorée Island and in St. Louis, followed by the Apostolic Prefecture of Senegal in 1763. Unlike the explorers, whose intentions were largely mercenary, the religious orders went to Africa in search of souls, not gold. Some were members of the foreign missions founded in Paris in 1664. Their activities in Africa inspired a highly successful book that stirred some controversy when it was published in 1776. The author, a certain Abbé Proyart, not only praised the

*But these proud herdsmen had no intention of parting with their* cattle *in exchange for* the glass beads *that other Africans found so irresistible.*

**Above**
After the caravels came the heavy ox-drawn carts of Dutch farming communities, who explored and eventually colonized the Cape hinterland. In some cases, white settlers pitched their tents alongside native huts, as this picture shows. The area was originally very sparsely populated, and the Dutch met with no resistance from indigenous populations.

qualities of the African natives, but also contrasted "the genuine acts of charity performed by the missionaries with the philosophers' purely verbal expressions of altruism."

### Cape Town, a "refreshment station"
On 25 March 1647, the *Nieuw Haerlem*, one of a fleet of Dutch trading boats on their way to East Asia, was shipwrecked in a storm in Table Bay. It was this shipwreck — one of many off the treacherous Cape — that was to lead to the creation of a new state on the southern part of the African continent. In 1651, after considering a report compiled by the shipwrecked crewmen, the Dutch East India Company sent Commander Jan Van Riebeeck out

to the Cape with orders to establish a refreshment station at the Cape for ships en route to East Asia. He landed in 1652 and within a week had begun work on the Fort of Good Hope. Thanks to its temperate climate and Van Riebeeck's determination, the Cape soon became a major agricultural center. Its rich, fertile soil was capable of producing anything that could be brought from Europe, including wine. The first vine was planted in February 1659, marking the start of wine growing activities in the southern hemisphere. What started as a refreshment station was to become the gateway to the colonization of the African interior. Shortly after the Fort of Good Hope was established, ships began arriving at the rate of five thousand every year, and the handful of local planters could no longer keep up with demand. Driven by the need for fresh supplies, especially livestock, reconnaissance expeditions led by Van Riebeeck set out to explore within a radius of 200 miles. However, the proud Khoikhoi herdsmen whom they approached had no desire to part with their valuable cattle — not even for the glass beads that other Africans had found so irresistible. Faced with this "refusal to cooperate," Van Riebeeck brought in Bantu slaves from Angola to farm in sparsely populated areas.

### Huguenots in Africa
In 1598, Henry IV of France passed the Edict of Nantes, granting religious and civil liberties to the Huguenots (French Protestants). Louis XIV's subsequent revocation of the edict in 1685 drove the majority of Huguenots into exile in Holland—where they were soon to play a part in the colonization of the future South Africa. Under

pressure from Van der Stel, who succeeded Van Riebeeck as Commander of the Cape, the Dutch agreed to invite the Huguenots to sail with them to the Cape to augment the white population. From April 1688 to May 1689, 175 Huguenots settled in a region specially set aside for them approximately seventy miles from Cape Town: the Franschhoeck ("French Corner") previously known as the Olifantschboeck ("Elephant Corner") because of the wild elephants that lived there. The small contingent of Huguenots could ill-afford the luxury of an insular language; Huguenot children were forced to learn Dutch. However, French names survived—witness the countless South Africans today with names such as Durand or De Villiers. For years, too, the Cape was surrounded by places called "Languedoc," "La Provence," "La Fortune," and "Terre de Luc." In the early 1700s, the pioneering Boers (farmers) and Trekboers (settlers who had trekked to new settlements to rear cattle) pushed northward, occasionally using force to drive back the indigenous population. Eventually they reached the river they named "The Orange" in honor of the Dutch Dynasty defeated by French revolutionary armies in 1794. This was the context for the arrival of the British, who took advantage of Napoleon's defeat in Europe to annex the Cape Colony.

### Slavery, the "original sin"

The critical factors for the formation of a new culture, with its own, developing language (Afrikaans) and with several separate "racial" groups, emerged in the 17th and 18th centuries. These "first occupants" assumed the right to remain separate, particularly since the lands first discovered had been sparsely populated, and this

**Above**
When Portuguese explorers put into what is now called Mossel Bay in 1488, they named it Angra dos Vaqueiros ("Bay of the Herders") because of all the cattle kept by the local people. These were the Khoikhoi, pastoralists or herders who were to prove of great importance to Europeans as suppliers of fresh meat and milk.

later served as a specious argument for the establishment of apartheid. But the white man's "original sin," as far as the Africans are concerned, was slavery: when the white man discovered Africa, he introduced the black man to slavery. The reality, however, is that the practice of slavery was not invented by the Europeans. Slavery, or to be exact, the trade in prisoners, had been practiced on the African continent long before it was discovered by European explorers.

What is commonly referred to as "the slave trade" — the transportation of black Africans across the Atlantic — was practiced from the 16th century until its abolition in the 19th century. The age-old traffic in slaves meanwhile continued on the east coast of Africa. Egyptians had been enslaving the Nubians since the times of the Pharaohs, and for centuries black slaves seized in West Africa were the main "commodity" traded across the Sahara. Human beings were a marketable product regularly exchanged for salt by Berber slave traffickers. In his travels though Africa, Ibn Battuta would frequently have passed caravans of prisoners on their way from the Mali Empire, then in its heyday, to Morocco. Slavery in Africa flourished until the early 20th century. However, the precise meaning of the word "slave" varied, and did not always involve chains and floggings. Large numbers of black women, especially Peules who were renowned for their beauty, were kept in harems. Black men were bought as reinforcements by every Muslim army, and although they were called "slaves," they enjoyed a relative freedom as soldiers. Depending on sex and age, slaves bought by the Arabs were used as cannon fodder, sex objects, or domestic servants. Slaves bought by the whites, on the other hand, were chiefly a source of labor.

Black communities also traditionally kept slaves. Long before the arrival of the Portuguese, many African societies with "kings" and hierarchical forms of government used slaves for difficult domestic tasks. As these local "kings" soon realized, the arrival of the Portuguese opened up lucrative business opportunities, including the sale of slaves. Just as there was once a Gold Coast (until Ghana became a republic in 1960) and still is an Ivory Coast, so the eastern Bay of Benin became the infamous Slave Coast featured on ancient maps. Initially then, there was no need for the Portuguese to explore further inland, since the demand for slaves could be supplied directly by the Africans. Only later would the *pombeiros*, African slavers who were often mulatto, go deep into Angola to supply the needs of their white masters. In the early days, the slaves were kept in boats at anchor. Later they were herded into slave forts along the coast while awaiting collection by the slave ships. It could take several months to build up a sufficiently large "cargo" on board, with the ship pulling into several slave ports along the coast. Long delays increased the death toll among the slaves and crew alike.

## European slave ports

With the development of plantations in the New World, a previously minor business activity soon became a flourishing industry. The slave trade was part of a global trading system known as the Triangular Trade. This involved "exporting" manufactured goods from Europe to the African west coast, where they would be

exchanged for slaves, then selling the slaves to planters in the Antilles or Louisiana, and finally buying tropical commodities with the proceeds and shipping those commodities back to Europe. This lucrative business helped to make the fortunes of some of today's most respectable European cities: Nantes and Bordeaux in France, and Bristol and Liverpool in England were all once thriving slave ports.

The exact numbers of Africans shipped overseas by the slave trade are hotly debated. The most recent, most dispassionate, estimates put the figure at somewhere in the region of twelve million from 1450 to 1870, with a peak of seven million in the 18th century. Of those seven million, some 2.5 million slaves were shipped by the British, 1.8 million by the Portuguese, 1.2 million by the French and 400,000 by the Dutch. Denmark, Sweden, and German towns on the Baltic played a more marginal role. In many cases, the traders were big commercial firms operating with public funds and private capital (the equivalent of today's government-controlled corporations). In France, these companies tended to be badly run, except for the Compagnie des Indes which did well in the early 18th century, shipping an average of two to three thousand Africans each year to the Antilles. The directors of this company, who included naturalist Michel Adanson, had a genuine interest in African natural resources, but they had no qualms about pursuing what they regarded as a legitimate business opportunity. It is also noteworthy that the traffic in slaves continued after it was officially abolished by many nations in the years between 1807 and 1833.

## Tragic crossings

By modern standards, the slave trade appears scandalous and astonishing, but it becomes easier to understand – though it never can be excused – by taking into account the harsh living conditions during these times. It is estimated that up to twenty-five per cent of the men, women, and children chained in the holds of the slave ships died before they reached their destination –

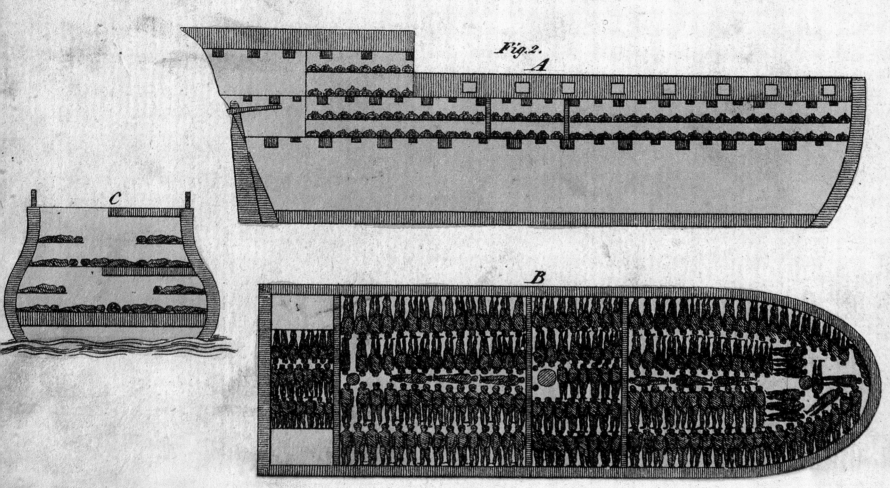

Fig.2.

There are two or three streets near Cancalli [a district in Cairo] where they sell **poor Christian slaves**. I have seen more than 400 of them there at a time, mostly black. They line them up against the wall, **stark naked** , with their hands tied behind their backs so that people can see them properly and make sure there is nothing wrong with them. Before being taken to market, so as to make them easier to sell, they are given a bath and their hair is brushed and artfully braided.

Bangles are slipped onto their arms and legs, and rings are hung from their ears and braids. Then they are taken to market to be **traded like horsemeat**, the girls with nothing but a scrap of cloth to cover their intimate parts. They may be **be examined by all and sundry**, handled, prodded, and poked, made to run and walk, speak and sing, show their teeth and exhale in case their breath should stink.

Before the deal is fully struck, in the case of a girl, she is taken aside and draped with a large sheet. Matrons, hired expressly for this purpose by the buyer, then proceed to **examine her intimately**.

If her virginity is intact, she is worth more.

Jean-Palerne Forésien, *Voyage en Egypt* (Travels in Egypt), 1581,
as quoted by François Renault and Serge Daaget, *Les Traites Négrières en Afrique*
(Slave Trading in Africa), Karthala, 1985

which was certainly not in the interests of their owners. Whether pure coincidence or poetic justice, an equivalent number of whites were employed by the slave trade, often risking their lives in inhospitable climates with no access to medical care. Some seventy-five per cent of the first French settlers in Saint Louis of Senegal died within a year of their arrival.

For all that, the shippers who traded in human flesh were regarded as right-thinking men with the slaves' best interests at heart. By shipping them out of Africa, people argued, the whites had saved the African natives from a far worse fate at the hands of cruel local despots, and because slaves usually received a proper Christian baptism, the Vatican did not formally condemn what it described as the "inhuman traffic in Negroes" until 1839. In the 15th and 16th centuries, the Christian world was largely unmoved by the plight of a heathen people from a remote continent. The Ethiopians were the only exception — probably because there had been Christians in Ethiopia (formerly Abyssinia) since Saint Fromence had spread the word there in the fourth century. Ethiopian women were said to be as beautiful as the Peules, and it was tragic to think of them for sale in the markets of Cairo.

MOI LIBRE

**Opposite, left**
In the 1770s, French illustrations displayed increasing concern for the plight of slaves torn from loved ones. With the French Revolution came the notion of the free African inspired by the French philosopher Jean-Jacques Rousseau (1712-1778). The African shown on the left is dressed as a French "sans culottes" (French revolutionary of the poorer class).

## The Signares of Gorée

The transatlantic slave trade was dependent on the principle of "natural" inequality. However barbarous and inhumane, it led directly to the practice of "voluptuous racial integration" started by the Portuguese: white men took black women into their beds. After months, sometimes years away from home, cut off from all contact with loved ones, the Portuguese could hardly fail to notice the charms of the African women, many of whom were strikingly beautiful, regardless of whether they were slaves.

Gorée Island, the French slave port (off the coast of Senegal) rapidly acquired a reputation as a place of "easy living," where a bevy of dark-eyed beauties waited to satisfy a man's every desire. Their mulatto daughters had lighter skin than their mothers and were even more attractive to the Europeans. These were the origins of the "Signares" (from the Portuguese "senora," for woman), wealthy businesswomen who eventually converted to Catholicism and founded the most famous dynasties, some of which still exist in Senegal. Still, African common-law wives and their offspring had no legal status until 1773, when "marriage Senegalese style" ("le mariage à la mode du pays") was officially recognized by the Devaulx government of Senegal.

## Birth of abolitionism

As we saw earlier, the French philosophers of the Enlightenment who wrote *L'Encyclopédie* had relatively little to say about Africa and even less about slavery. Under the heading *"Nègre"* (Negro), it is only mentioned that the treatment of slaves in the "French islands of America" was the subject of a lengthy royal edict forbidding their employment on "Catholic days of rest."

In fact, not until the end of the 18th century was a more enlightened view adopted, starting in England and following in France at the time of the French Revolution. Just as the ethics of the slave trade came into question a renewed interest in the exploration of, and travel within, the African continent emerged. In 1788, this led the wealthy amateur scientist Sir Joseph Banks, who had previously accompanied Captain Cook's expedition to the South Pacific, to found the African Association for Promotion of Travel and Discovery in Africa, which was absorbed by the Royal Geographical Society in 1831. In its brochure, the Society noted with dismay that "nearly one third of inhabited lands, including practically the whole of Africa, remain undiscovered." The African interior beckoned, but for some explorers at least, the ultimate goal was also to wipe out the slavery that persisted within African communities themselves.

**Following double page**
At the end of the Napoleonic Wars, France and England did at least agree to put an end to slavery. This picture shows British troops on 18 November 1815, announcing the Treaties of Paris signed by allied forces abolishing the slave trade. The British would pursue their ambitions in Africa in the name of commerce, mixing little with local populations but respecting local customs. The French, on the other hand, like the Portuguese, felt they were on a mission to civilize, a duty that was bound to require some integration.

# II

# The call of Timbuktu

*The Niger, or "Negro River," was the longest of the rivers shown (mainly for decorative purposes) on early maps of western Africa. Nobody had charted the course of this mighty river, which flows more than 2,500 miles from Guinea to Mali. Some said it fed into the Nile, and others, such as Leo the African, claimed that it flowed southward. According to Ptolemy, the Niger flowed through a desert. Just to complicate matters, the Africans themselves knew the Niger by various names, unaware that what they called the "Joliba" or the "Kourra" were in fact one and the same river. In the late 1800s however, the members of the African Association in London sensed that the Niger river basin was a key element of west African geography encompassing, as it was later confirmed, a host of fascinating regions. Not least of these was the mysterious, enigmatic Timbuktu.*

*Mungo Park, just twenty-three years old but **not lacking in self-confidence**, eagerly agreed to lead an expedition sponsored by the African Association **to trace the course of the Niger**.*

This confusion surrounding the Niger is hardly surprising when one considers all the twists and turns in its great, northward-curving passage through present-day Guinea, Mali, Niger, and Nigeria. After rising on the northwest side of the highlands of Guinea, the baffling Niger appears to dive toward the very heart of Africa, then skirts Timbuktu before reaching the Gulf of Guinea at the end of its 2,500-mile journey. It would take Europeans thirty years to appreciate the full scale of the Niger, and even longer to recognize the Niger river delta, first noted by 16th-century Portuguese explorers around Port Harcourt, as the point where the river splits into a network of outlet streams.

Sir Joseph Banks, Head of the African Association, was a rich landowner as well as an explorer. Among his acquaintances was James Dickson, a corn chandler with a passion for botany. Dickson's brother-in-law was a certain Mungo Park (1771 – c. 1806) a qualified physician and seventh of thirteen children from a modest Scottish farming family. Dickson introduced Park to Sir Joseph Banks, who found the young man a position as ship's surgeon on board an East India Company ship. Upon his return, Park, just twenty-three years old at the time but not lacking in self-confidence, eagerly agreed to lead an expedition sponsored by the African Association to trace the course of the Niger. He left for The Gambia, where he learned Malinke (the local language), picked up some tips from slave merchants, and recruited a small team including a native interpreter named Johnson and Demba, a manservant. In December 1795,

Park left Pisania (The Gambia) on horseback, with enough food to last two days, a donkey each for Johnson and Demba, various trinkets to use for barter, a sextant, a thermometer, two rifles, two pairs of pistols, underwear, and of course, an umbrella.

**Negro Kingdoms**

What Park referred to as the "Negro Kingdom" in fact consisted of several smaller "kingdoms" that were often at war with each other. The issues involved ranged from cattle theft to land division but the principal cause was the animosity between the Moors (Muslims of North Africa) and the Negroes to their south. Travelers crossing from one kingdom to another were forced to pay "rights of passage," which soon exhausted Park's supply of bartering "currency." He also found that the Moors were generally hostile to anyone with a Christian name, and that the others could not understand how "any man in his senses would undertake so dangerous a journey, merely to look at the country and its inhabitants." Because of these local conflicts, Park was soon forced to deviate from his planned route and travel by way of several Negro "kingdoms" to the north, all with long-forgotten names. The welcome he received varied according to the personality of the local king. Park's account of the expedition is largely focussed on the relations he forged with these often unpredictable and sometimes downright hostile men.

For example, Park wrote that the King of Kaarta treated him with "great kindness" and showed concern for his safety. In stark contrast, the Moorish sovereign of Ludamar was "tyrannical

It is impossible for me to forget the disinterested charity and tender solicitude with which many of **these poor heathens** (from the sovereign of Sego to the poor women who received me at different times into their cottages... **sympathized with me in my sufferings**...and contributed to my safety. This acknowledgment, however, is perhaps owed more specifically to the female part of the nation. Among the men, as the reader must have seen, my reception, though generally kind, was sometimes otherwise.

Mungo Park, *Travels in the Interior Districts of Africa*, 1799

*In July 1796, after a series of adventures, and pushing his exhausted horse,*
## Park finally reached the River Niger.

and cruel" and held the explorer prisoner in a pigsty "out of derision for a Christian." In the end, it was the sovereign's wife Fatima who took pity on Park, now "in great distress for want of water." There was also the king of Bondou, who, despite his friendly welcome, actually had designs on Park's coat and umbrella, believing they would enhance his status and serve for "all public occasions."

### The Niger "as broad as the Thames"

All Park's traveling companions had by this time fled except for Demba, who remained with him to the end. Finally, in July 1796, at the end of a series of adventures, and pushing his exhausted horse, Park reached the River Niger: "The long sought for majestic Niger, glittering to the morning sun, as broad as the Thames at Westminster… I hastened to the brink and, having drunk of the water, lifted up my fervent thanks in prayer, to the Great Ruler of all things, for having thus far crowned my endeavours with success." Shortly afterward, the explorer entered the kingdom of Sego, capital of Bambarra (present day Mali) where King Mansong refused to see Park but sent him a present of five thousand cowrie shells "to relieve a white man in distress." These shells served as local currency and would prove extremely useful later on.

Although Park had originally intended to press on to Timbuktu, under the circumstances he decided to turn back. He was now weak with fever and especially anxious to avoid the neighboring kingdom of Maniana, where the inhabitants were said to be "cruel and ferocious" and likely to dispose of their enemies by way of "disgusting banquets of human flesh." He wrote: "I am well aware that the accounts that the Negroes give of their enemies ought to be received with great caution; but I heard the same account in so many different kingdoms, and from such a variety of people, whose veracity I had no occasion to suspect, that I am disposed to allow it some degree of credit."

The return journey was not without incident and included an attack by bandits, who stripped Park of everything except his precious journal. By the time he arrived back in The Gambia his hosts were convinced he was dead. He returned to London in December 1797 "having been absent from England two years and seven months."

**Below**
Cowrie shell necklace. Cowrie shells were traditionally used as money in many parts of Africa and Asia. When Mungo Park ran out of money and was forced to use his last remaining uniform buttons, he was given a bag of cowrie shells by King Mansong — who was more hospitable than most. Explorers in western Africa later imported large quantities of cowrie shells from Zanzibar, where they were cheaper. "It was like the old alchemist's dream come true," said one explorer. "Suddenly we could manufacture gold."

**Left**
Mungo Park had occassion to thank certain "good" Africans for their hospitatlity. But Gaspard-Théodore Mollien, who visited west Africa some years later having survived the ship wreck of the "Medusa," received a rather more mixed welcome from local residents on the Atlantic coast.

## Fact replaces fiction

*Travels in the Interior Districts of Africa* was published in London in 1799. It was the very first eyewitness account of a number of regions previously unknown to Europeans. The only other explorer to have led an expedition into the African interior from The Gambia was the British officer Major Daniel Houghton, who had never returned and was presumed to have been killed by the Moors. Although Park had not achieved all of his goals — the course of the Niger remained uncharted, and Timbuktu was no less mysterious — the details he provided did much to replace fiction with fact. Furthermore, he paved the way for further exploration by showing that, armed with a little practical psychology where the natives were concerned, a white man could return alive from darkest Africa.

## Meeting with a white man

Park's ability to observe human behavior was remarkable, and there is nothing even remotely idealized about his comments on the people he met. As he himself wrote about the Moors, "manners and general habits of life will be best explained as incidents occur in the course of my narrative." Accordingly, his observations are entirely based on his own experience. For example, he writes of a joyful family reunion: "From this interview I was fully convinced, that whatever difference there is between the Negro and European, in the conformation of the nose and the colour of the skin, there is none in the genuine sympathies and characteristic feelings of our common nature." He also notes that seeing a white man for the first time could come as quite

a shock: "Two Negro horsemen, armed with muskets, came galloping from among the bushes: on seeing them I made a full stop; the horsemen did the same; and all three of us seemed equally surprised and confounded at this interview. As I approached them, their fears increased, and one of them, after casting upon me a look of horror, rode off at full speed." However, once they had recovered from the initial shock, people were generally friendly and as curious about Park as he was about them. One old man, for example, asked Park for a lock of his hair, claiming that it would "give the possessor all the knowledge of white men... I had never before heard of so simple a mode of education, but instantly complied with the request." Even the wily Moors, who were substantially less naïve than the Africans to the south, showed an endless fascination for Park's buttons: "I was employed, dressing and undressing, buttoning and unbuttoning, from noon to night." The king's wives demonstrated a similar curiosity, inspecting "every part of my apparel, [they] searched my pockets and obliged me to unbutton my waistcoat and display the whiteness of my skin: they even counted my toes and fingers, as if they doubted whether I was in truth a human being."

While Park refrains from any comments that might have been considered improper at the time, his words suggest an admiration for the joy and "graceful attitudes" of native women. On the other hand, he makes no secret of his dislike of the Moors: "They are a subtle and treacherous race of people... with singular ideas of feminine perfection. The gracefulness of figure and motion, and a countenance enlivened by

*Park had determined* that the Niger flowed toward the Gulf of Guinea and saw the river as his best chance of return. *He would never be seen again.*

**Above**
London publisher John Murray (1778–1843), the first to publish the works of Jane Austen and Lord Byron, and founder in 1809 of the Tory-leaning *Quarterly Review*. In 1832 he published the Lander brothers' account (which he bought for 1,000 guineas). In the 20th century, *John Murray, Albemarle Street, London W1* would become famous for its excellent travel guides bound in elegant red and gold.

**Opposite**
Hippopotami near the mouth of the River Luala. Painting by Thomas Baines (1820–1875).

expression, are by no means essential points in their standard"; even Moorish nuptial ceremonies lack that "mirth and hilarity which take place at a Negro wedding." He also claims that the Moors "take every opportunity of cheating and plundering the credulous and unsuspecting Negroes." Indeed, as our explorer knew full well from meeting caravans of slaves captured by the Moors, the treatment of these unhappy souls was inhumane. He was less outspoken on the subject of the African "domestic slave," whose treatment is governed by certain rules established by tribal custom "which it is thought dishonorable to violate."

At the end of the chapter Park expressed an opinion that would later be criticized by abolitionists. "In the present unenlightened state of [the African] mind" he wrote, the effect of abolishing the slave trade "would be neither so extensive or beneficial, as many wise and worthy persons fondly expect."

### Park's mysterious death

His courage and exploits having captured the public imagination, Park was now an established hero who felt he had won the right to speak his mind. His only regret was that he had not seen his mission through to the end. On his return to England, he married Allison Anderson in 1799 and settled down to work as a doctor in a small town in Scotland. But he soon tired of domestic life, and when the chance of a new expedition came his way, Park accepted without hesitation. His family learned of his decision only a few days before he was scheduled to depart.

The opportunity was offered by the Colonial Office in London, which had already done much to effect the colonization of Indian Bengal. Its attentions now were increasingly focused on western Africa, which, despite the presence of the French in Senegal, offered lucrative trading possibilities.

Park was formally in charge of an official mission, given the rank of colonel, and assigned a regiment of thirty-four soldiers from the British garrison on Gorée Island (temporarily taken from the French in 1800). Their departure coincided with the start of the rainy season, and consequently malaria and dysentery decimated the troops. Park had in any case found the soldiers to be an added complication, as they prevented him from approaching his previous contacts. By the time he reached Bambakoo, on the Niger, only six soldiers

But here **a fresh evil arose**, which we were unprepared to meet. An incredible number of **hippopotami** arose very near us, and came plashing, snorting, and plunging all round the canoe, and placed us in imminent danger…. Our people, who had never, in all their lives, been exposed in a canoe to such huge and formidable beasts, trembled with fear and… absolutely wept aloud…. Our people tell us that these formidable animals frequently upset canoes in the river, when every one in them is sure to perish. These came so close to us, that we could reach them with the butt end of a gun. When **I fired** at the first, which I must have hit, every one of them came to the surface of the water, and pursued us so fast over to the north bank, that it was with the greatest difficulty imaginable we could keep before them. Having fired a second time, the report of my gun was followed by a **loud roaring noise** and we seemed to increase our distance from them.

Richard and John Lander, *Journal of an Expedition to Explore the Course and Termination of the Niger,* 1832

remained. Undaunted, Park pushed on toward Sego, where Mansong (who was still king) gave him permission to build a type of schooner. In a letter to his wife that was taken back to The Gambia by messenger, Park assured her that he had every confidence of reaching the ocean in safety, even though his regiment by this time had dwindled to only four soldiers.

He had by now determined that the Niger flowed toward the Gulf of Guinea and saw the river as his best chance of return. He would never be seen again. According to Park's African interpreter, who was dispatched by the British to investigate in 1810, the explorer and his companions drowned in the Bussa rapids after being attacked by Indians. For years, Park's family refused to believe this story, and in 1827 his eldest son Thomas set off for Africa to find out what happened once and for all. Tragically, he died of fever before ever reaching Accra.

Three years later, two British brothers, Richard and John Lander, embarked by canoe from Lagos, in Nigeria, on an official government mission to determine the course of the lower Niger. Another of their objectives was to solve the mystery of Park's death. For two boys from a modest family of Cornish innkeepers, this was an excellent opportunity to climb the social ladder. Their aspirations would have been shared by numerous other explorers of the period, many of whom were of humble origins. In 1830, having explored upriver from Bussa (the area from which Park had disappeared), the Lander brothers headed downstream, where they were taken hostage by the Ibo shortly before reaching the mouth of the Niger. Their ransom having been paid by the captain of a British ship, Richard and John arrived safely back in London. They could now confirm that the lower Niger flowed toward the Gulf of Guinea. It did not flow, as previously suggested, toward some mysterious lake, or toward the Sahara, the Nile, or the Congo. So ended one of the great geographical mysteries of the time, opening up interesting trade possibilities in Nigeria for Liverpool shippers. Meanwhile, Park's death remains unexplained.

## Mollien, a born survivor

Africa in the early 1900s remained a dangerous destination in every sense. On 2 July 1816, the French frigate *Medusa* ran aground on the treacherous Arguin Bank off the northern coast of present-day Mauritania. What followed ranks among the most infamous of all sea disasters: 150 men and women were abandoned on a makeshift raft and all but fifteen drowned, were murdered by pirates, or were eaten by cannibals. Their plight is immortalized in Théodore Géricault's pivotal work, *Scene of a Shipwreck* (now known as *Raft of the Medusa*). One of the few survivors was Gaspard-Théodore Mollien, who, at twenty-two years old, had volunteered to join a resettlement expedition to Senegal. France had recently regained its holdings in Senegal (Gorée Island and Saint Louis), which had been captured by the British in 1815, following Napoleon's defeat at Waterloo. Mollien, whose father had died prematurely, had been forced to work from an early age, but he had grown tired of his job as a clerk at the Naval Ministry. The expedition to Senegal was the opportunity he had been waiting for.

After yet more setbacks, including a hostile reception from the Moors and the British when the rescue boat reached shore, Mollien finally reached Gorée Island. Two years later, with the official backing of the governor of Senegal, Mollien undertook a mission to explore the African interior and investigate the source of the Niger. He left on 28 January 1818 with an African interpreter and a donkey loaded with supplies provided by the French Administration. By the time he returned to Dakar a year later, he had explored the Fouta-Djalon highlands and visited Timbuktu, in mind if not in body, thanks to the endless tales of the Peul people – who were never actually able to take him to the place itself. Mollien's account of this expedition, *Voyage dans l'intérieur de l'Afrique aux sources du Sénégal et de la Gambie*,

published in 1820, describes the Moorish influence and the spread of Islam throughout the region.

### Two Englishmen on the banks of Lake Chad

The British Colonial Office had meanwhile set its sights on remote Islamic shores and in 1822 launched an expedition to Bornou, in Chad. The team leaders were Dr Walter Oudney, a naturalist, and two British Officers, Captain Hugh Clapperton and Major Dixson Denham. They left from Tripoli, where the British Consul was on good terms with the local Pasha. Denham, who is described as consummately British, was fully determined to wear both his nationality and his religion on his sleeve by dressing in European clothing, come what may. Perhaps it was something of this quality that led to a rather combustible relationship between Denham and his fellow officer Clapperton; they had not chosen each other as travelling companions and feuded constantly in the testing circumstances. Early explorers enjoyed strictly

**Below**
Clapperton arriving in Maroua, a town in the most touristic area of present-day Cameroon. He was so impressed by the scenery that, despite falling ill on the first expedition, he returned to Nigeria, only to die from dysentery on 13 April 1827 near Kano, in the arms of his white servant.

*In 1816, **the young René Caillié** landed in Saint-Louis, Senegal, fully determined to makeup for his unpromising start in life*

rudimentary comforts and the enforced proximity was often as bad, if not worse, than the isolation. Shortly after leaving Libya, Denham and Clapperton quarreled in front of an embarrassed Oudney. Worse still, they then wasted time and money composing lengthy diatribes that had to be sent by messenger—at great expense—to the British Colonial Office. Each insisted that he would only take orders directly from the British government. In one letter to the Admiralty, Clapperton claimed that the loss of Denham would be "a saving to his country for Major Denham could not read his sextant, knew not a star in the heavens, and could not take the Altitude of the sun."

Despite the endless rows, the Bournou Mission, as it was officially known, made reasonably good progress. The men advanced through the Tuareg and Toubou territories, following the tracks left by the slave caravans, along the way passing a macabre group of chained corpses. Then, in January 1823, came the first signs of vegetation, much to the relief of all concerned, followed on February 4 by the discovery of an immense lake. Lake Chad, beckoned the British to be the first white men to bathe in its waters. In true jingoistic spirit, still hugging himself with pleasure over Napoleon's defeat in 1815, Denham suggested calling it "Lake Waterloo."

There were more reasons for satisfaction in Kouka, former capital of Bournou, where the Sultan received them in the traditional manner: seated on a silken cushion inside a bamboo cage, which served to distance his noble person from

his baser subjects. Denham and Clapperton were well received, and their mission had been a success, but they nevertheless remained as irreconcilable as ever and decided to go their separate ways. Denham ventured deeper into Bornou and discovered the Chari River, which feeds Lake Chad. Clapperton and Oudney headed west, discovering the majestic Mandara Mountains, with the Islamic stronghold of Maroua nestling in the foothills, north of present-day Cameroon. Shortly afterward, Oudney fell mortally ill but Clapperton, despite being in poor physical shape himself, was able to continue. After reaching Kano, a fortified town in present-day Nigeria, he went to the caliphate of Sokoto (west of Kano, also in Nigeria) where the Sultan was well disposed toward whites. By the time he met up with Denham again on the return journey, Clapperton was too sick to fight, and the two reached London together in January 1825. In 1828, the "terrible twins" published two separate accounts of their travels under the same title, *Narrative of Travels and Discoveries in Northern and Central Africa (in the years 1822, 1823 and 1824)*.

### An appeal from the Société de Géographie
When the ill-fated *Medusa* left France in 1816, it was sailing in convoy with another French ship, *La Loire*, that would later rescue some of the survivors. On board was a sixteen-year-old cabin boy destined to become the first European to set foot in the legendary city of Timbuktu. His name was René Caillié (1799-1838) and, like Mollien, he had had an inauspicious start in life.

His father, a baker from Aunis, in western France, had been sentenced to twelve years hard labor in 1799 following vague accusations of theft. Left to fend for himself from birth, the young René soon tired of life as an apprentice shoemaker in provincial France and set off to see the world. On this first visit to Senegal in 1816, he tried to join up with a British search party looking for Mungo Park but failed and returned to France. He spent the next few years saving money for a return trip, to Senegal, which he made in 1824. Upon his return to Africa, he learned basic Arabic and familiarized himself with the everyday Muslim customs of the Moorish riverside populations.

The French had only recently retaken possession of Senegal and the young colony was in the grips of exploration fever, fed by reports such as this one from the governor of Senegal, Colonel Schmaltz: "I have traveled far and wide and seen a great many countries, but I have never seen a country more beautiful and better suited to major enterprise than Senegal. The banks of our river look every bit as fertile as those of the Ganges and are equally capable, I am sure, of producing whatever crops we may care to grow." Back in France, meanwhile, the growing fascination, bordering on obsession, with Timbuktu would change Caillié's life forever.

In 1821, the geographical engineer Edmé-François Jomard (who had taken part in Napoleon's expedition to Egypt) founded the Société de Géographie in Paris. The 217 founding members included six French academicians,

*The legendary 12th-century city of* Timbuktu, *in the vicinity of the River Niger, was* a meeting point *point for African populations and nomadic Berber and Arab peoples, Muslims and pagans alike. It was a focal point for trade, with* gold and slaves *being the most common commodities.*

plus essayists, novelists, journalists, engineers, doctors, clergymen, and civil servants. One of the aims of the society was to encourage adventurers and researchers to explore unknown lands, and like the African Association in London (founded in 1830), its principal target was Timbuktu. Its members had read Ibn Battuta's and Leo the African's somewhat vague descriptions of the legendary 12th-century city that lay in the vicinity of the River Niger. They knew it as a center for trade between the Arab North and southern Africa, with salt, gold, and slaves being the most common commodities. They also knew that, at its height in the mid-15th century, Timbuktu was the celebrated center of Islamic learning, home to several thousand scholars and three world-famous mosques (Jingereber, Sidi Yaya, and Sankoré). But the fact remained that no European in living memory had ever set foot there.

In 1824, the Société de Géographie published an announcement in its magazine offering a generous reward to the first European explorer to return alive from Timbuktu. The terms of the reward say a good deal about the spirit of the period: "This reward is offered to any traveler who shall return unscathed from his perilous enterprise having gathered vital information on the geography, output and trade of the country in question. The description of the indigenous populations shall include details of their customs, ceremonies, dress, laws, religions, diet, illnesses, skin color, shape of face, and hair type."

### Caillié's long walk

When the Governor of Senegal saw this announcement, he immediately sent a copy to Caillié, a man known to be passionate about travel. By the late 1500s, forty-two Europeans, including twenty-five Englishmen and fourteen Frenchmen, had tried to reach the legendary city. None of them had succeeded and some had died in the attempt. Out of these forty-two intrepid explorers, nineteen had departed from northern Africa and twenty-three had embarked from the west coast of sub-Saharan Africa. Caillié chose the latter option.

He departed from present-day Guinea on 19 April 1827, with an African guide, four porters, and various items of equipment, including two sextants, a medicine kit, writing paper to make notes, silk handkerchiefs, scissors, mirrors, and three one-guinea pieces to use as barter. He also took an umbrella, partly to protect himself from the sun and the rain, but mainly as a symbol of authority: other than the whites, who had

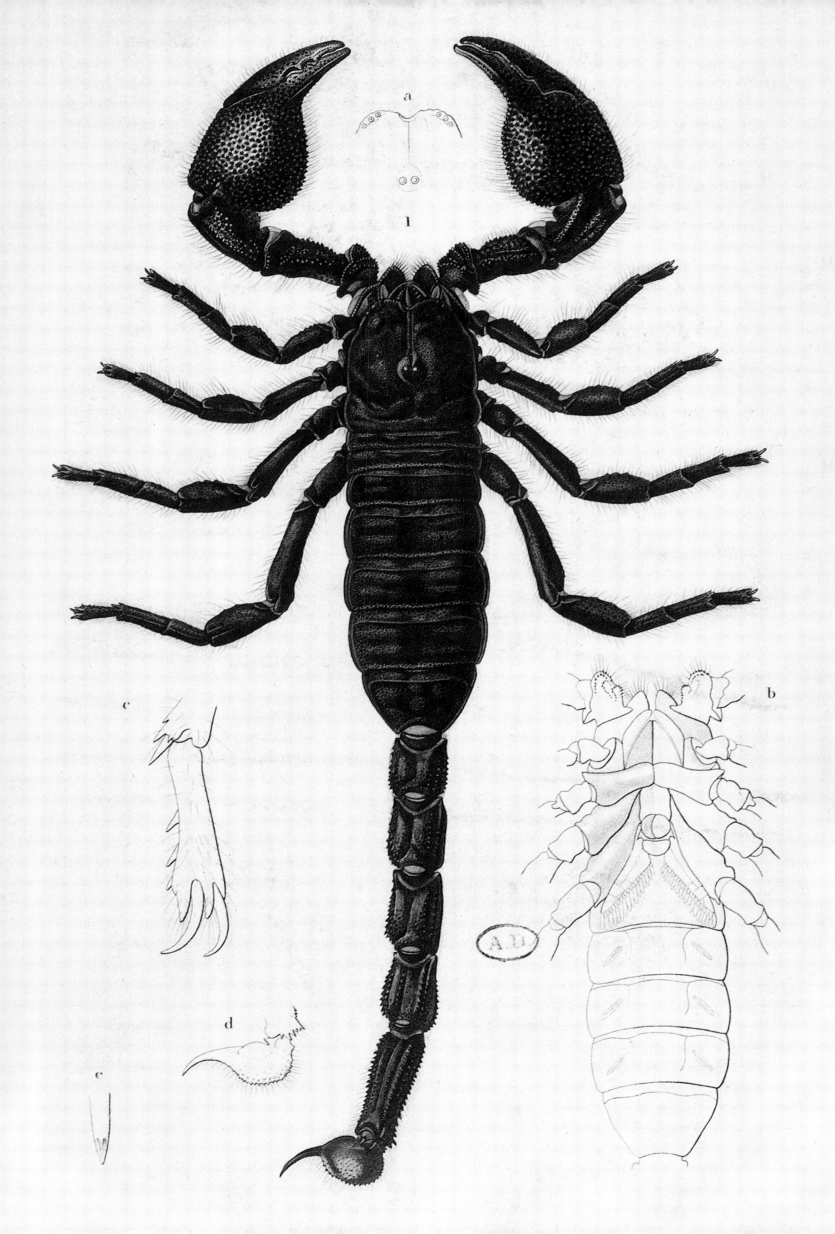

*He was **outraged** by what he saw now: "In that part of Africa,
the sheer scale of the loathsome trade in
human flesh **was an insult to humanity.**"*

invented them, only chiefs ever carried umbrellas. Caillié eventually gave his to a rich Moor from Tafilalet (southeast Morocco) to thank him for his hospitality.

Caillié had decided to travel in disguise, mainly to avoid arousing suspicion about his rudimentary Arabic, but also to win sympathy. He posed as an Egyptian from Alexandria who had been carried off to Senegal as a child by Napoleon's men and was now trying to find his way home. Later, when his skin had turned such a deep shade of brown that nobody would ever have guessed he was a European, he pretended to be a Moor — and as a consequence he was forced to observe the strict fasting regimen during Ramadan.

Progress was slow across the savanna, and during his journey Caillié developed scurvy. In addition, his feet were covered in blood and there was a loose bone in his palate. Close to death, he stopped in a place north of the present-day Ivory Coast, where "a good old negress" nursed him back to health. Six months later, he joined up with a caravan of Malinke traders and set off for Djenne.

## A disappointing legendary city

The ninth-century city of Djenne, about 190 miles south of Timbuktu, was a striking spectacle to behold (and still is), with its well-preserved mud architecture and imposing mosque, but Caillié was in no mood to notice. He was entirely preoccupied with reaching his goal and increasingly annoyed with the the Negroes, to whom, he wrote, "time costs nothing." As it turned out, though, they did offer him the chance to sail toward Timbuktu in a dugout, which was vastly easier than walking.

On 20 April 1828, almost exactly a year since he had left Guinea, Caillié finally reached Timbuktu, having covered more than nine hundred miles on foot, but was sorely disappointment with what he found. As he would later reveal in the account of his travels, this battle-scarred city, ravaged by invasions, was far less magnificent than what he, and most European explorers, had envisioned. Leo the African's famous palace were nowhere to be found, and the most exotic items now on sale in the central market were French rifles made in Saint-Etienne.

Caillié also found that he was not the first European to enter the "Forbidden City." Major Alexander Gordon Laing, who had left Tripoli in 1825, had been murdered by Tuaregs shortly after his arrival. Clearly it was not advisable to linger in Timbuktu, and after spending just thirteen days writing up his notes, Caillié began the journey home. He had decided not to retrace his steps, but rather to return by way of the Sahara to prove that he really had been to Timbuktu. Unknown to him, the worst was yet

*"Generally speaking, people throughout the interior of the Sudan believe that we live on small islands surrounded by seas, and that we Europeans would like nothing better than to take over their country; they regard it as the most beautiful place in the Universe."*

**Below**
Illustration from the first edition of Caillié's account, with the caption "Mr Caillié meditating on the Koran and taking notes." The original caption, "Mr Caillié taking notes while pretending to meditate on the Koran," was amended by the author when he saw the final galleys, out of respect for Muslim sensibilities.

to come: the route across the desert would prove even longer and expose him to people far more hostile than the inhabitants of Timbuktu.

A Moroccan, who had taken Caillié under his wing in Timbuktu, arranged for him to join a caravan of Moorish traders, disguised as a Muslim, whereby he left the city by camel. However, he soon fell out with the Moors, who treated him badly and would certainly have sold him as a slave had they discovered he was a Christian. Although no stranger to the horrors of slavery since leaving Guinea, he was outraged by what he now witnessed: "In that part of Africa, the sheer scale of the loathsome trade in human flesh was an insult to humanity."

Caillié finally reached Morocco by way of Tafilalet, and to his great relief saw Portuguese ships off the coast of Rabat—his first sight of Europeans in months. But the "French consular agent," to whom he appealed for help, took one look at

Caillié's appearance, his feet bloody from the rigors of his journey, and sent him packing. Caillié rode to Tangiers on a donkey, where, to his amazement, the French Consul welcomed him with open arms and "not the least sign of disgust." The consul was Jacques-Denis Delaporte, a member of the Société de Géographie who had exchanged letters with Jomard. Delaporte quickly grasped what his fellow countryman had achieved, and after seeing to his medical needs arranged for Caillé's return on a warship. On arrival in France, he was forced to spend some time in quarantine in Toulon (a port town in the south of France) before continuing to Paris.

**The Legion of Honor for the son of a convict**

When the members of the Société de Géographie debriefed Caillié, they could see immediately that he was telling the truth. "There is not the slightest hesitation when he answers, no matter how much we question him," writes Jomard. "He knows where he went, when he went there, what mountains and rivers he crossed, how far he traveled, and what routes he took. What more do we need? We have seen his original, hand-written notes, penciled in secret in the desert under cover of his Arab robes or hidden from view behind a rock or bush."

Thus it transpired that René Caillié, the son of a convict, became a national hero. He was decorated with the Legion of Honor and received two cash prizes: the original reward offered by the Société de Géographie plus an additional sum from the Naval Ministry. The account of his travels, published in 1830, was

**Opposite**
Elephant towing the *Victoria*,
an original illustration from
Jules Verne's *Five Weeks in a
Balloon*. Verne was a great
admirer of Caillié and a
prominent member of the
Société de Géographie in
Paris, source of vital
material for his novels.

printed by the Imprimerie Nationale and dedicated to King Charles X.

While the goal of the expedition was to find Timbuktu, the place itself only accounts for a single chapter in Caillié's book. The remaining pages include a map, notes by the Société de Géographie, and a wealth of previously unpublished information on west African regions and the opportunities they offered to France, especially in Guinea ("rich farming country, good for crops"). Jomard probably rewrote some of the passages for stylistic reasons while retaining all the immediacy of the original text. The book was also the first to describe the appearance and application of certain plants, such as the sesame leaves used by the Africans to flavor their "soups." Before setting off, Caillié studied African botany in the northern Senegalese town of Richard-Toll, where French horticulturists were conducting field trials. Although he collected specimens throughout the trip, to his disappointment none of them proved suitable for analysis.

Chief among its virtues, Caillié's book provides unprecedented insight into what African people thought at the time, particularly about white people. "Generally speaking, people throughout the interior of the Sudan believe that we live on small islands surrounded by seas, and that Europeans would like nothing better than to take over their country; they regard it as the most beautiful place in the Universe." Caillié also

By means of various bribes, including
*"a pair of English razors,"*
*Barth survived six months in Timbuktu.*

recorded some of the rumors arising from the transatlantic slave trade. One day, for instance, Caillié was asked by an African if it was true that Christians ate their slaves — people knew that prisoners taken by slave ships across the Atlantic were never seen again. By way of response, Caillié replied that, in the opinion of white men, "all men are equal in the eyes of the law." Clearly, despite his father's harsh sentence, Caillié remained a loyal patriot who felt it was his duty to spread the Republican message.

In 1830 Caillié married and went to live in the provinces, where he hoped to feel more at ease than in Parisian society. But a return to normal life seemed impossible, and despite the allowances he received from several benefactors, Caillié soon ran into financial difficulties. He grew increasingly bitter and, like Mungo Park, yearned for a new expedition. It was not to be: in 1838, aged just 39, René Callié died suddenly of pneumonia. A much wider recognition of his contributions came after his death; many writers of the time presented him as a shining example to young people. In 1867, for example, Jules Verne's Dr. Ferguson in *Five Weeks in a Balloon* makes the following comment as he flies over Timbuktu: "Now if Caillié had been born in England, he would have been honored as the most intrepid explorer of modern times, equal to Mungo Park himself! But in France, no one fully appreciates his true worth." To be fair though, Caillié was venerated in France, where he was considered a forerunner of humanitarian colonization. His accomplishments inspired many worthy books thought eminently suitable for school prizes. By some fortunate coincidence, Jomard, Caillié's benefactor and the founder of the Société de Géographie, was also the head of the Ministry of Education in Paris.

## Barth, distinguished Arabist and energetic walker

The German explorer, Heinrich Barth (1821-1865) would display even greater ingenuity and insight than his predecessors in the ranks of early African exploration. He would also play a major role in promoting the efforts of the British Anti-Slavery Society in London. Barth was born in Hamburg on 16 February 1821, the son of a German merchant family. By the age of thirty he was an accomplished linguist, fluent in English, French, and Arabic, with a distinguished academic record in the fields of history, geography, botany, archaeology, and medicine. In the course of his studies, he had traveled to various parts of the Mediterranean before returning to work as a lecturer (Privatdocent) at Berlin University. But he was beginning to tire of his academic existence and longed for the globetrotting days of his youth. In 1850 he was invited to join a British expedition to Lake Chad headed by the explorer James Richardson, a member of the British Anti-Slavery Society. The team of men set off from Tripoli in 1850, across the Fezzan (southwest

Libya, in the Sahara) followed by the Aïr Massif (north-central Niger, also in the Sahara). A series of severe setbacks, including threats of ambush and torrential rainfall rarely experienced in Saharan regions, forced the team to disband. Barth, who was in good physical good shape and an energetic walker, decided to proceed alone. He traveled disguised as a Muslim by the name of Abd el-Krim and spoke such good Arabic that it was impossible to tell he was an imposter. His route by way of Chad-Sudan and Nigeria-Sudan was much the same as Clapperton's twenty-five years earlier.

Barth reached Timbuktu in September 1853 after wading endlessly through the marshes that flanked the Niger. He was not the first white man to pass through its gates but he probably holds the record for the one who stayed there the longest. Thanks to an enlightened *marabout* (a Muslim holy man from North Africa) and by offering bribes,

including "a pair of English razors," Barth survived six months in Timbuktu. In fact, he was on such good terms with his Muslim friend that he even admitted to being a Christian.

## From salt mines to harems

The account of Barth's 12,500 mile journey, published in German and English in 1858, testifies to the outstanding intellectual abilities of a man with a genius for observation and a passion for accuracy. *Travels and Discoveries in North and Central Africa in the Years 1849-1855* features maps drawn to an astonishing degree of precision, remarkably detailed illustrations, good-humored meteorological observations, and well substantiated facts that give a clear picture of complex patterns of human settlement. In language that is easily understandable to the western reader, Barth tempered his insatiable curiosity with a sober style and a critical attitude. He willingly sampled African

**Above**
Barth wrote of delicate huts surrounded by lush vegetation, and friendly smiling people who lived in harmony with the animals.

food to enable him to describe it first-hand. He debunks reports of gold exports from Timbuktu by studying the actual quantities of gold shipped overland and by water. His account of the salt mines (salt having always been the main commodity bartered by the riverside kingdoms of the Niger) is so precise that it could be based on actual geomorphological data. For all that, Barth was no dispassionate observer, and he freely expressed his indignation at the "rude labors" of the Africans contrasted with the idleness of the Europeans.

His descriptions of harems are equally enlightening. He writes that the Sheik of Bornou had only twelve wives but that the Sultan of Baghirmi returned from his military expedition with no less than forty-five exotic beauties. The vizier El Hadj Bechir, on the other hand, was the proud proprietor of a four-hundred-woman harem — he collected women, so he said, as other people collected stamps. While each one was interesting in her own right, collectively they allowed him to memorize all the different specimens of the human race. Whenever the name of an unknown tribe came up in conversation with Barth, the vizier would immediately dispatch his men to find the missing female specimen. For reasons of propriety no doubt, the chapter on harems features none of the detailed sketches found elsewhere in Barth's account.

In other ways, he is rather more open on the subject of women than his predecessors, while still maintaining that he always kept his distance. He explains, for instance, that the daughters of local potentates would consult him for all

manner of reasons, often to ask for "medicines" for imaginary ailments.

One of these "princesses," whom he describes as shapely and appealing, was delighted when he commented on her beautiful eyes, a western compliment unusual in Africa. We also learn how curious the women were to see inside the author's tent and how surprised they were to find no lady friend there.

### The night of the long-awaited caravans

Germans retained a fascination with Timbuktu and were at the forefront of Saharan exploration despite the growing French influence in western Africa. In the early 1870s, Gustav Nachtigal (1834-1885), a medical doctor, traveled to the Fezzan and explored the Tibesti (northwest Chad). In 1879, the German African Association sent Oscar Lenz (1848-1925) on a reconnaissance mission from Tangiers to the Atlas Mountains in Morocco. Lenz then received permission to press on to Timbuktu, on the border between the Sahara and western Mali. "For the man who travels to Timbuktu, it is as important to arrive there as it is to reach Lhasa, capital of Tibet, after a long and difficult journey to the heart of Asia." This quote is taken from Lenz's book *Reise durch Marokko, die Sahara und den Sudan* (Travels in Morocco, the Sahara, and the Sudan), which was dedicated to that "master of African scientific exploration, Heinrich Barth."

The town that Caillié had found so disappointing became the focus of French military influence in West Africa. It remained a

**Above, left**
Having sent his camels, horse, servants, and luggage across first, Barth was filled with excitement at crossing the Niger, "this celebrated stream, the exploration of which had cost the sacrifice of so many noble lives."

**Above, right**
Barth described Kano as the "real capital of Negroland," full of clay huts and houses. The houses featured a secluded second-story where light and air were sacrificed for the sake of complete privacy.

*One of these "princesses," whom he describes as shapely and appealing,
was delighted when he commented on her* beautiful eyes,
*a western compliment unusual in Africa*

magical, mysterious place well into the 1930s, the inspiration for an entire generation of authors, including French journalist and social reformer Albert Londres (1884-1932) and the short-story writer Paul Morand (1888-1976). In his *Terre d'ébène*, Londres describes Timbuktu as "the city of pleasure on the night of the long-awaited caravans" where the mystery "is something you feel rather than see." Morand meanwhile could think of no catchier title than *Paris-Tombouctou* for his account of travel in Senegal, the Sudan, Guinea, and the Ivory Coast.

## Loneliness and loss of identity

From these early 19th-century adventurers who blazed a trail of glory to Timbuktu arose the popular conception of the African explorer. But Park, Caillié, Mollien, Clapperton, and Barth were all quite different characters. Park and Caillié were young people, determined to better their social positions at any price, while Captain Clapperton and Barth were middle-class professionals in search of new horizons. Park would succumb to the temptation of a second expedition and die in the attempt, while Mollien preferred to hang up his walking boots and eventually become French Consul in Havana. No matter their differences in character, their experiences were quite similar. They all endured extreme physical hardship and

**Above**
Mid 19th-century illustration of a young girl from Timbuktu offered for sale to a customer in Tripoli. In explorers' accounts, artists had to avoid suggestive illustrations that were likely to "compromise" the authors, but they made up for it with highly imaginative engravings depicting "Negresses" in Arab harems.

*"Of all the maps and geography books people lent me," wrote Caillié,*
*"the map I found most fascinating was the*
*map of Africa, on which all I could see were spaces*
*marked 'unknown territory.'"*

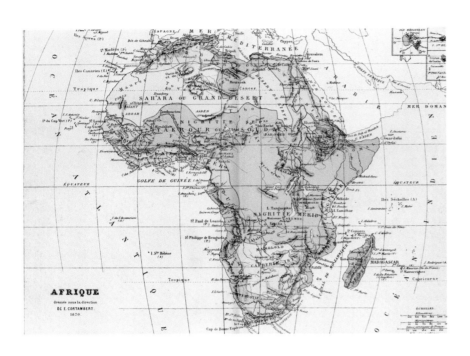

exhausting treks; some even survived malaria.
All of them were in danger of being discovered
and took endless pains to hide their telltale
journals ("I always carried my own death
warrant" wrote Caillié). Some, disguised as
Muslims, suffered from Christian identity
crises; all of them heaved a huge sigh of relief
when they returned to the bosom of their
fellow whites. Caillié's heart leapt when he set
eyes on the Portuguese boat off the coast of
Rabat; Mollien, although on dry land,
exclaimed, "Land at last!" when he reached the
European base in the heart of West Africa. And
yet not one of these pioneering spirits could be
accused of racism. With increasing colonization
expeditions became more organized. Future
explorers would have their share of physical
hardship — but never that terrible loneliness

suffered by their predecessors, all of whom had
met each other and later described their
meetings with sultans or "kings," some
friendlier and more generous than others.

## Childhood tales

Regardless of their level of education, all of these
explorers shared a passion for books and owed
their wanderlust to early childhood tales — not
surprisingly they all published accounts of their
travels once safely back home. "Of all the maps
and geography books people lent me," wrote
Caillié, "the map I found most fascinating was the
map of Africa, on which all I could see were spaces
marked 'unknown territory.' That was when I first
decided to make my name as a great explorer."
Although thoughts of territorial conquest never
crossed their minds, all of these explorers, from
Park to Barth, were loyal patriots. In his
dedication to Charles X, Caillié wrote: "I strove
for that most glorious of all rewards: the honor
of presenting the king with the fruits of my
explorations to unknown lands, where famous
travelers lie buried." Barth meanwhile ended his
book with the hope that the fruit of his labors
would be to the greater glory of the German
race. Some explorers included in their accounts
words of thanks for the help and support of
fellow Europeans, as Lenz wrote: "I shall never
forget the courteous, spontaneous welcome I
received in French bases in Senegal."

# III

# The magic of the Nile and the Zambezi

*The Nile was even more mysterious than the Niger. Where was the source of that mighty river, lifeblood of Egypt, which was once the home of a great civilization? The Nile had maintained its aura of mystery since the first century A.D., when Nero's expedition to find its source had been defeated by the marshlands in Nubia. Nobody knew whether the "Mountains of the Moon," which Ptolemy claimed to be source of the Nile, were real or imagined. Were they the stuff of legend, or observable objects recorded by some adventurous sailor to Africa's eastern reaches? The only way to find out, since the cataracts at Aswan made it impossible to sail up river, was to set off from the east African coastline*

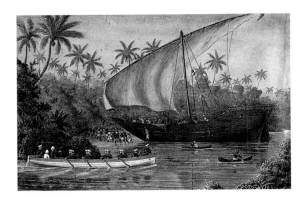

*The supplies included a quantity of*
## *fake pearls* *to pay the "rights of passage"*
*levied by the various kingdoms.*

**In the late 18th century, Scots aristocrat** James Bruce (friend of the French naturalist Buffon) had found his way to Lake Tana in the highlands of Ethiopia.

**Preceding double page**
The Victoria Falls on the Zambezi River, by British artist and explorer Thomas Baines (1822-1875). Having made his name with the paintings inspired by his trip to Australia, he subsequently accompanied Livingstone on his reconnaissance mission to the Zambezi.

**Above**
Small craft near Zanzibar, where the Arab dhows were far more elegant than the British steam boats. Steamers were nevertheless an important asset for explorers in the first half of the 19th century, dramatically cutting the time previously taken by sailing ships to transport vital equipment from Europe.

**Opposite**
Burton, seen here, insisted on posing with a book in his hands. Many explorers were widely read and regarded reading as an essential part of their adventurous existence.

He claimed at the time, rather precipitously as it turned out, that the river flowing south out of the lake was the Nile. This was, in fact, the Blue Nile, the Nile's principal tributary. The members of the Royal Geographical Society (which had absorbed the African Association in 1830) were far from convinced by Bruce's hypothesis. It offered no explanation for the annual flood pulse in the Nile Delta from July to October — which would cease only with the completion of the Aswân Dam in 1970. Such dense water masses could form only in a basin much larger than Ethiopia, encompassing vast stretches of land with an intense rainy season.

### Two British explorers amidst the Arab traders

Enter Captain Sir Richard Francis Burton (1821-1890), a veteran captain in the East India Company army, formidable linguist, and explorer *par excellence*. In 1858, this talented man (the hero of the film *Mountains of the Moon*) would discover Lake Tanganyika, narrowly missing Nyanza (Lake Victoria), the source of the Nile. The expedition he led with another British Officer, Lieutenant John Hanning Speke (1827-1864), is described in William Harrison's *Burton and Speke* and in Burton's own account of his travels, *The Lake Regions of Central Africa: From Zanzibar to Lake Tanganyika* (1860).

With his thorough knowledge of Arabic (he would later translate the *Arabian Nights*), Burton had managed to infiltrate Mecca disguised as an Afghan pilgrim. He soon realized that Arab slave dealers and ivory traffickers were his passport to the African interior — nobody else knew how to get there. Not a man to let his conscience interfere with his passions, Burton decided to join them.

In 1857, with the blessing of the British Foreign Office and the Royal Geographical Society, Burton left from Bagamoyo, opposite Zanzibar, on an expedition to find the source of the Nile. With him were his friend John Speke, an expert marksman whose skills would prove invaluable; a guide provided by the local Sultan; approximately one hundred porters; and a donkey for each of the Europeans. The supplies included a quantity of fake pearls to pay the "rights of passage" levied by the various kingdoms.

Burton felt at ease with the Arab traders and admired their lavish ways. In his account, he praised the merchant from Zanzibar who knew what it was to do without and spared no expense to alleviate the stresses and strains of the journey. He remarked on the striking contrast "between the open-handed hospitality and the hearty good-will of this truly noble race, and the niggardness of the savage and selfish African — it was heart of flesh after heart of stone." Burton's racism would later draw comment from Madame Loreau, his French translator, who attributed it to "all the tribulations he had suffered."

At the Ziwa the regular system of kuhonga, or blackmail,
so much dreaded by travelers, begins in force. Up to this point all the
chiefs are contented with little presents; but in Ugogo
tribute is taken by force, if necessary. None can evade payment;
the porters, fearing lest the road be cut off to them in future, would
refuse to travel unless each chief is satisfied; and when a quarrel arises
they throw down their packs and run away...
The chiefs [always reply] that as they never expected to see white
faces again, it was their painful duty to make the most from them.
The kuhonga, however, is not unjust. In these regions it forms
the customs-dues of the government: the sultan receives it nominally,
but he must distribute the greater part among his family and
councilors, his elders and attendants.

Richard Burton, *Lake Regions of Central Africa* (1860)

*"When unfit for exercise, we are borne in hammocks,* **slung to long poles**, *and carried by two men at a time."*

Which is not to say that Burton was insensitive to the charms of certain Black women, to whom he refers as "charming pet animals" worthy of modeling for any sculptor.

Thanks to "introductory letters" from people with influence, the expedition advanced through East Africa, where "made roads, the first test of progress in a people, are unknown. The most frequented routes are like goat-walks, one to two spans broad, trodden down during the traveling season by man and beast, and during the rains the path, in African parlance, 'dies,' that is to say, it is overgrown with vegetation." When the men were too weak from fever to walk, they rode on the donkeys. When even that became impossible they were "borne in hammocks, slung to long poles, and carried by two men at a time." Otherwise, the daily routine varied little: "The usual occupations are the diary and the sketch-book, added to a little business.... Dinner at four P.M. breaks the neck of the day." The menu, depending on the food available, ranged from "leathery goat-steak to fixings of delicate venison, fatted capon, and young Guinea-fowl." (The game birds were shot by Speke.) On 13 February 1858, Burton and Speke finally sighted Lake Tanganyika "as it lay in the lap of the mountains, basking in the gorgeous tropical sunshine."

## A Lake for Queen Victoria

The expedition made camp at Ujiji — a site that would later become famous as the meeting place of explorers Stanley and Livingstone. Burton then learned that a little river called the Rusizi flowed out of Lake Tanganyika toward the north.

He surmised that it might be the headwaters of the Nile. After a difficult journey in two dugout canoes, the two explorers made it to the river only to find that it flowed into and not out of Lake Tanganyika. Plainly, the river could not be the origin of the mighty Nile.

Burton and Speke then separated. Burton was too exhausted to continue and stayed behind in Tabora. Speke went on to explore the area north of Tanganyika, in search of the *bahr* ("sea" or "lake") described to Burton by Arab traders. Six months later his perseverance was rewarded when he discovered "a magnificent sheet of water," which he promptly named Lake Victoria,

in honor of the Queen of England.

Speke and his companions did not map the extent of Lake Nyanza (its original African name); instead he accepted without doubt that he had found the source of the great Nile River and returned to Tabora. "At length my companion had been successful," Burton would write later. "His 'flying trip' had led him to the northern water, and he had found its dimensions surpassing our most sanguine expectations. We had scarcely, however, breakfasted, before he announced to me the startling fact that he had discovered the sources of the Nile." Burton remained highly skeptical, believing Speke's discovery to be "an inspiration" and told him so.

By the time they reached Zanzibar, their friendship was at an end. It received the final death blow when Speke returned to England ahead of Burton and promptly informed the Royal Geographical Society of "his" discovery. Burton meanwhile insisted that the source of the Nile lay toward Mount Kilimanjaro. The issue divided explorers throughout Europe, compelling the Royal Geographical Society to put an end to the controversy once and for all: Speke was commissioned to lead a new expedition to Lake Victoria and bring back

**Above**
Captain James Grant looking down on Uganda from a bluff. This Scottish officer, who won the *Victoria Cross* for valor during the Indian Sepoy mutiny of 1857, was unanimously awarded the 1864 medal by the Royal Geographical Society in London for his exploits in southern Africa. In Africa, as in Asia, he regarded himself first and foremost as a servant of the Crown.

The man sent to find them was
*Sir Samuel White Baker,* a British explorer
with the time and money to indulge his passion for
geographical research. His expeditions were all self-financed.

incontrovertible proof of his claim.

In 1860, he and a fellow East India Company army officer, James Grant (1827-1892), departed from Zanzibar following the route of the 1857 expedition. They reached Lake Victoria in July 1862. After a detailed reconnaissance, Speke identified the source of the Nile as a large waterfall at the lake's northern end.

As he had expected, the waters were flowing out of the lake and not toward it. Whatever Burton might think, Speke was confident that he had been right from the start.

### The source of the Nile explained

Speke now wanted to return to civilization and report that the mystery of the Nile had been solved. Grant, meanwhile, was busy converting a certain King Kamrasi (in present-day Uganda) who had expressed an interest in the Bible. Speke persuaded his friend that God could wait, and the pair set off to find the shortest possible route out of darkest Africa.

Back in Khartoum, Grant and Speke were presumed missing, and the British Consul had dispatched a friend of Speke's, Sir Samuel White Baker (1821-1893), to find them. Baker was a British explorer with the time and money to indulge his passion for geographical research. His expeditions were all self-financed. In the account he wrote of his mission, Baker described his emotional meeting with Speke and Grant in February 1863. It was off the shore of Gondokoro, a city on the banks of the Nile some six hundred miles south of Khartoum: "My men rushed madly to my boat, with the report that two white men were with them who had come from the sea! Could they be Speke and Grant? Soon I met them in reality. Hurrah for old England! They had come from the Victoria N'Yanza, from which the Nile springs... The mystery of ages solved... We were shortly seated on deck, and such rough fare as could be hastily prepared was set before these two ragged, care-worn specimens

of African travel, whom I looked upon with feelings of pride as my own countrymen."

A few weeks later, Speke cabled London from Cairo stating that: "The geographical question of the sources of the Nile is explained." Burton continued to advance his own theory regarding Tanganyika, and a special meeting was convened by the Royal Geographical Society to hear both cases. However, on the day before he was due to address the association, Speke, a crack shot, was killed in a hunting accident in England.

## Florence Baker "upon her ox"

Samuel Baker was convinced that, despite the map he had been given "with characteristic candour and generosity" by Speke and Grant, "a most important portion still remained to be determined." While he did not doubt that Lake Victoria was the source of the Nile, it was evident that the river "must derive an additional supply from an unknown lake." As he would later write in his account, "one leaf of the laurel remained for me."

African exploration at the time was an exclusively male domain. Victorian social mores dictated that a woman's place was in the home, and female emancipation was very much in its infancy. Florence Baker (1842-1916) was one of the few women to challenge these assumptions and to win a distinguished place in the field of African exploration. Other pioneering women explorers were Alexandrine Tinne (1835-1869), Dutch explorer of the Nile River and North

Africa, and the British Mary Kingsley (1862-1900) who made her mark in equatorial Africa. Florence Baker was born in Hungary in 1842 as Florence Barbara Maria Finnian von Sass. Her family was killed in war, and when she was seventeen, left alone to fend for herself, Florence ended up in a Turkish slave auction in Bulgaria. (Slavery persisted in Europe well into the 19th century.) She was bought by her future husband, Samuel White Baker, and from then on the two were inseparable. Although Baker refers to his "wife" throughout his book, he and Florence were not formally married until their return to Europe in 1861.

The Bakers left Gondokoro by boat and sailed southward, joining a slave caravan where the Nile was no longer navigable. In the early days of their expedition, Baker, an expert shot like Speke, indulged himself by shooting giraffe and observing wild animals that he had never seen before. But things grew progressively more difficult as savanna gave way to malaria swamps, and the porters deserted one after another. To add to their troubles, King Kamrasi displayed none of the cordiality he had shown to Grant. He insisted on his customary right to "borrow" Florence for one night, offering Baker one of his own beautiful ladies in exchange. Baker took offense and threatened to shoot the king, whereupon he and Florence departed on oxen, by this time their sole means of transport. Some time later, Florence collapsed from heatstroke, much to the alarm of Baker's men, who started

**Above**
Baker in discussions with natives chiefs (left), and visiting a village with Florence (right). Although Baker was eventually knighted by Queen Victoria for his courage, Florence was not received by the Queen until the couple were married. The Empress of India's fame spread to the Black Continent, where certain British explorers did not hesitate to pass themselves off as her sons in a bid to impress the Africans.

to dig her grave. "The sudden wild cry of a hyena made me shudder as the horrible thought rushed through my brain that, should she be buried in this lonely spot, the hyena would... disturb her rest."

Baker need not have worried – his wife made a full recovery. The couple finally reached the area where the natives confirmed Baker's theory about a second "unknown lake." The morning of 14 March 1864 brought incontrovertible proof: "a sea of quicksilver" bounded by "great ranges of mountains" on the border between present-day Uganda and Zaire. Baker christened it Lake Albert in memory of Queen Victoria's recently deceased husband.

In more recent times, the lake was renamed after the Congo's second president, Joseph Mobutu. For good measure, in honor of the president of the Royal Geographical Society in London, Baker gave the name Murchison Falls to the explosion of water where the Nile bursts through a 130-foot ravine on its way to the Mediterranean.

## Whiskey for a Ugandan king

It took many months for the Bakers to return to London via Khartoum and Cairo. On their return trip, they found King Kamrasi in better spirits, and Baker even complimented the chief on his "beautiful and highly cultivated" kingdom, with its surrounding "immense fields of sweet potatoes." The explorer decided that a celebration

was in order, so he tried his hand at distilling "potato whiskey" from sweet potatoes: "Not having tasted either wine or spirits for nearly two years, the sudden change from total abstinence... had a marvelous effect." It seems that the "hot toddy" Baker drank everyday eventually cured him of fever, while Kamrasi "got drunk so quickly upon the potent spirit, that he had an especial desire to repeat the dose." So impressed was the king with Baker's whiskey still that it became the cornerstone of "King Kamrasi's Central African Unyoro Potato-Whiskey Company, Unlimited."

## The enigma is finally solved

Baker was convinced that he had unraveled the mystery of the African Great Lakes Region and assembled all the pieces of a particularly complex puzzle. "Bruce won the source of the Blue Nile," he writes, "Speke and Grant won the Victoria source of the great White Nile; and I have been permitted to succeed in completing the Nile Sources by the discovery of the great reservoir of the equatorial waters, the Albert N'yanza, from which the river issues as the entire White Nile." Not everybody was as convinced as Baker, and it would fall to two legendary explorers, David Livingstone (1813-1873) and Henry Morton Stanley (1841-1904), to bridge the missing links – such as Lakes Edward and George, which were discovered by Stanley between 1875 and 1889. Today, it is generally agreed that the Nile has

several sources rather than one. According to the *Encyclopedia Britannica*, the furthest headstream is the Kagera River, which rises in the highlands of Burundi near the northern tip of Lake Tanganyika and then flows into Lake Victoria. The Nile proper, however, rises from Lake Victoria, and begins near Jinja, Uganda, on the north shore of the lake. The northward stretch of the river, known as the Victoria Nile, enters the shallow Lake Kyoga (Kioga) and flows out in a westerly direction before entering the northern end of Lake Albert. A small, pyramid-shaped monument on a mountain in Burundi marks the spot where the "real source" was discovered in 1938 by the German explorer Burkhart Waldecker. The Germans remained fascinated by the enigmatic Nile long after they were driven out of Burundi by the Belgians in 1919.

## The snows of Kilimanjaro

Professional explorers were not the only ones who were determined to conquer the Dark Continent. In the first half of the 19th century, Protestant missionaries of various denominations went to Africa to spread the Word, but also to conduct research of their own. Their first port of call was South Africa, more hospitable than west or equatorial Africa, and not yet touched by Islam. In 1814, John Campbell of the London Missionary Society traced the Harts River and explored the Orange as far as Augrabies Falls.

The source of the river was first discovered by the French Protestant minister Thomas Arbousset in a mountain he named "Mont-aux-Sources" (Mountain of Sources). Arbousset was also a pioneer in the field of ethnography. He spent some twenty years with the Basotho tribe in Lesotho studying their ways and their language — into which he translated the Bible — and transcribing their poems. But the master of East

**Following double page**
Photograph taken c. 1889 of a cave at an altitude of more than 5,500 feet on Mount Elgon, on the border between Kenya and Uganda.

*The best way to spread the Word,* **in Livingstone's opinion,**
*was to discover waterways and land routes that would eventually lead*
*to the establishment of trading posts and the promotion of trade.*

### Livingstone, early missionary days

While on campaign in Egypt in 1798, Napoleon Bonaparte decided that the simplest way to obtain reinforcements was to ask the Sultan of Darfour for "two thousand strong, energetic black slaves over the age of sixteen." The arrival of the slave caravans, bringing fresh supplies of female concubines, was always eagerly awaited by Napoleon's men. By the 19th century, European governments were no longer prepared to tolerate slavery in Africa. In 1808, America passed a bill banning the import of slaves from other countries (though the institution of slavery itself continued through the Civil War), which effectively wiped out the former system of "Triangular Trade." In 1815, the Congress of Vienna, Great Britain, and France officially banned the slave trade. The principle of slavery itself was outlawed by the British in 1824, followed by the French in 1831, then Spain and Portugal some years later. However, a black-market in slaves continued well past this time. It is one thing to pass a law and quite another to police it. Lithographs, photographs, and paintings of slave ships being captured by Britain's Royal Navy illustrate the long struggle against the illegal slave trade.

One of the duties of the missionaries sent out to Africa was to inform the native population that the transatlantic slave trade had been forbidden by law. It was an important duty for the Scots missionary David Livingstone, who was destined to become the most celebrated British explorer of all time. Born on 19 March 1813, in Blantyre, Scotland, David Livingstone was the son of devout but humble militant Presbyterians. (The

African languages was the German missionary Johan Krapf, stationed near Mombasa from 1837 to 1855, who translated the Bible into Swahili. In 1848, a fellow German missionary, John Rebman, was the first European to see the snow-capped summit of Mount Kilimanjaro. Although his story at the time was greeted with derision by the geographic community, it was confirmed by Krapf in 1849.

On the 15th there was a procession and service of the mass in the **cathedral**; and wishing to show my men a place of worship, I took them to the church, which now serves as the chief one of the See of Angola and Congo. There is an impression on some minds, that a **gorgeous ritual** is better calculated to inspire devotional feelings, than the simple forms of the Protestant worship. But here the frequent genuflexions, changing of positions, burning of incense, with the priests' backs turned to the people, the laughing, talking, and manifest irreverence of the singers, with firing of guns, etc, did not convey to the minds of my men the idea of adoration. I overheard them, in talking to each other, remark that "they had seen the white men **charming their demons**"; a phrase identical with one they had used when seeing the Balonda beating drums **before their idols**.

David Livingstone, *Missionary Travels and Researches in South Africa (1857).*

*By the 19th century, European governments were no longer prepared to tolerate slavery in Africa.*

capital of Malawi was later named after his birthplace.) At the age of ten, Livingstone was put to work in a cotton mill, but he continued his education in night school and won a scholarship to study medicine and theology at Glasgow University. In 1838, he was accepted by the London Missionary Society, and two years later he was ordained as a missionary. He arrived in Cape Town on 14 March 1841.

When Livingstone arrived in Cape Town at the age of twenty-seven, relations between the British and the Boers had become strained. The Dutch settlers had become British subjects against their will in 1815, when Holland ceded its colony to Great Britain, and from that point on the Dutch played only a marginal role in Africa. Missionaries with abolitionist ideals were inevitably unpopular with white colonists who kept native servants in near-slave conditions. The tension between Livingstone and his white "compatriots" soon became unbearable. He and his wife Mary Moffat, whom he married shortly after his arrival, decided to leave Cape Town and set up home with their children in the north. In the years that followed, they had succeeded in converting not one single African. In 1849, Livingstone won a prize from the Royal Geographical Society in London, for his account of the discovery of Lake Ngami south of the Zambezi River. At that point he decided to change his vocation from pastorship to exploring. The best way to spread the Word, he thought, was to discover waterways and land routes that would eventually lead to the establishment and promotion of trade. "Sending the Gospel to the heathen must… include much more than is implied in the usual

picture of a missionary, namely, a man going about with a Bible under his arm…. The promotion of commerce ought to be specially attended to…. Success in this, in both Eastern and Western Africa, would lead… to a much larger diffusion of the blessings of civilization than efforts exclusively spiritual and educational confined to any one small tribe."

### Lianas the size of boa constrictors

In 1852, after taking Mary back to Cape Town, where she boarded a ship returning to England, the pastor-turned-explorer set out on a long trip to Angola. His objective was to prove that the Atlantic Ocean could be reached from the depths of southern Africa. With him went some thirty men, most of them Makololos from a tribe

**Above**
John Campbell used ox-drawn wagons to take the load off porters, but problems arose when it came to crossing a river.

**Following double page**
"We have a good view of the mass of water… as it leaps quite clear of the rock, and forms a thick unbroken fleece all the way to the bottom. The snow-white sheet seemed like myriads of small comets…" Livingstone watching the Victoria Falls.

on the borders of the Zambezi with whom he was on good terms. The party ran into difficulties, however, when the time came to leave the canoes and waterways and start the trek through the forest: "The forests became more dense as we went north. We traveled much more in the deep gloom of the forest than in open sunlight. No passage existed on either side of the narrow path made by the axe. Large climbing plants entwined themselves around the trunks and branches of gigantic trees like boa constrictors, and they often do constrict the trees by which they rise, and, killing them, stand erect themselves."

The column nevertheless reached the River Kasaï (which lent its name to a province in present-day Zaïre), where Livingstone had to satisfy various "impudent" chiefs who demanded goods in exchange for the right to cross their territory. The "pearls" he had brought with him were not enough — he was forced to give up his last penny to a man named Katendé (no doubt an early ancestor of those civil servants who still live by baksheesh). All the same, he had some kind words for the local people: "I did and do feel grateful to these poor heathens for the promptitude with which they dashed in to save, as they thought, my life."

On 1 May 1854, Livingstone and his Makololos finally reached Luanda, which had been a Portuguese settlement, with a firmly established tradition of Portuguese Catholicism, for more than a century. The Protestant Livingstone spent a few months resting in Angola, where he drafted his report for the Royal Geographical Society. In

it he admits that the regions in question were just too inaccessible to think of establishing a trade route. Nevertheless, the expedition did allow him to chart regions formerly unknown to the British. In September 1855, he embarked on the return trip to Cape Town, but he then abruptly decided to push further down the River Zambezi, toward Portuguese Mozambique on the Indian Ocean.

### "Smoke that sounds"

His most spectacular discovery, on 17 November 1855, was the thundering, billowing waters of the River Zambezi, thrown up into the air like a "great jet of vapor." From a distance the waters looked exactly like smoke and were called "the smoke that sounds" by his Makololo bearers, who refused to proceed in canoes. But Livingstone pressed on, through what he describes as a landscape of unimaginable beauty: "It had never been seen before by European eyes; but scenes so lovely must have been gazed upon by angels in their flight." Eventually he

came to an island "situated in the middle of the river, and on the edge of the lip over which the water rolls." Peering down, Livingstone saw "a large rent which had been made from bank to bank of the broad Zambesi." From it gushed a torrent "a thousand yards broad" that leaped down more than three hundred feet into an abyss and then escaped through a channel two hundred feet wide.

After naming the falls after Queen Victoria, Livingstone left the Zambezi headed for Portuguese Mozambique. He arrived in the port of Quelimane in May 1856, having traveled some 6,250 miles — on foot, by boat, mounted on an ox, or carried in a hammock — and crossed Africa from the Atlantic to the Indian Ocean.

His account of his expedition, *Missionary Travels and Researches in South Africa*, was published in London in 1857; it sold 50,000 copies in England alone and was translated into many languages. The rich and leisured loved it, businessmen devoured it, and humanists deplored what it revealed about slavery. Protestant missions, however, felt that

**Above**
Dreamlike painting by Thomas Baines of a meeting between an elephant and the *Ma Robert*. Livingstone was alarmed at the scale of the ivory trade in Zanzibar and regarded elephants as a species in peril.

*As the steamer wheezed its way* **through malaria swamps infested with crocodiles,** *Livingstone's men renamed it the Asthmatic.*

Livingstone the missionary was now totally eclipsed by Livingstone the explorer. But the die was cast: Livingstone was appointed British Consul at Quelimane and "commander of an expedition for exploring eastern and central Africa, for the promotion of Commerce and Civilization with a view to the extinction of the slave-trade."

### An asthmatic steamer among the mosquitoes

Livingstone left Liverpool on 10 March 1858, together with his younger brother Charles, who had recently returned from the United States where he had studied cotton cultivation.

This expedition, infinitely better organized than the explorer's previous solo journeys, featured a "portable" paddle steamer, the *Ma Robert*, and an impressive list of supplies. In addition to the Livingstone brothers, there were five other British men (including a doctor and the painter Thomas Baines) and about sixty bearers.

Departing from the banks of the Zambezi River in September, the men headed for the spectacular Kebrabasa rapids (now Cabora Bassa) where the river forces its way through the mountains. From there, they sailed up the River Shiré (a tributary of the Zambezi) in the *Ma Robert* to explore reports of a great lake north of Mozambique. As the steamer wheezed its way through crocodile-infested malaria swamps, Livingstone's men renamed it the *Asthmatic*.

### No end to the "devilish traffic in human flesh"

Finally, on 16 September 1859, the expedition reached Lake Nyassa (Malawi), an immense expanse of water approximately 11,000 square miles in area. It soon became apparent that the "devilish traffic in human flesh" was still thriving. Slaves were regularly shipped from Zanzibar to Mozambique by Portuguese slavers, who took no heed of the treaties signed by Portugal. In his account, Livingstone reserved none of his indignation over the continued slave traffic in Africa, not only in Mozambique but throughout the East Coast: "One small vessel on the Lake would have decidedly more influence, and more good in suppressing the slave-trade, than half a dozen men-of-war on the ocean. By judicious operations, therefore, on a small scale inland, little expense would be incurred, and the English slave-trade policy on the East would have the same fair chance of success, as on the West Coast." On one occasion the expedition successfully frightened off the black slave drivers "armed with muskets, and bedecked with various articles of finery," escorting "a long line of manacled men, women, and children.... They were thus left entirely in our hands and knives were soon busy at work cutting the women and children loose. It was more difficult to cut the men adrift, as each had his neck in the fork of a stout stick, six or

**Below**
The convoy of prisoners encountered by Livingstone, whose books always featured illustrations that highlighted the persistence of the slave trade.

*"My father" explained Bennett, "has made [the New York Herald] a great paper, but I mean to make it greater. I mean that it shall be a* news paper *in the true sense of the word. I mean that it shall publish whatever news will be interesting to the world at no matter what cost."*

seven feet long, and kept in an iron rod which was riveted at both ends across the throat." The Livingstones claimed in their account that slaves captured in East Africa were bound for sugar plantations on the Île de Réunion. The island continued to receive shipments of slaves, euphemistically known as "contract workers" or "coolies" until 1864. In their joint account, *Narrative of an Expedition to the Zambezi and Its Tributaries*, the Livingstones would nevertheless pay tribute to Napoleon III for banning slavery: "Of all the benefits which the reign of Napoleon III has conferred on his kind, none does more credit to his wisdom and humanity than his having stopped this wretched system."

When he returned to London in 1864, David Livingstone received a hero's welcome, but his relations with other explorers had grown very strained. People found him increasingly moody following the death of his wife on the Zambezi in 1862 and many objected to the comments he made in his new book. Livingstone, however, was convinced that he had a divine mission to put an end to slavery — he was also far from sure that the sources of the Nile had been fully explained. He returned to the Lake region in 1868 but lost his way somewhere east of Lake

Tanganyika. For the next three years, he was presumed missing, probably murdered by slave drivers in Zanzibar.

**An exclusive for the New York Herald**

Henry Morton Stanley, the fabled journalist–explorer, was the man who eventually found Livingstone. Born John Rowland in Denbigh, North Wales, he had been cast off by his family and emigrated to the United States, where he was adopted by a wealthy American whose last name he took. After training as a journalist, Henry Stanley made his made his name as a press correspondent for the *New York Herald* in Abyssinia and Spain. In 1869, he was recalled on "important business" by the newspaper's young and ambitious owner, James George Bennett. "My father" explained Bennett, "has made [the *New York Herald*] a great paper, but I mean to make it greater. I mean that it shall be a news paper in the true sense of the word. I mean that it shall publish whatever news will be interesting to the world at no matter what cost."

And what was it that the whole world, including America, found so interesting at the time? African

"My father" explained Bennett, "has made [the *New York Herald*] a great paper, but I mean to make it greater. I mean that it shall be a news paper in the true sense of the word. I mean that it shall publish whatever news will be interesting to the world at no matter what cost."

**Above**
One of many portraits of Stanley in warrior mode. He never posed without his rifle.

**Above and opposite**
Stanley's worn-out pith helmet and trekking boots.

**Below**
Annotated map drawn up by Livingstone.

**Right-hand page**
"Hottentot [sic] girls dancing," a plate from Thomas Baines's *Travels in the Interior of South Africa* — strikingly like a Matisse.

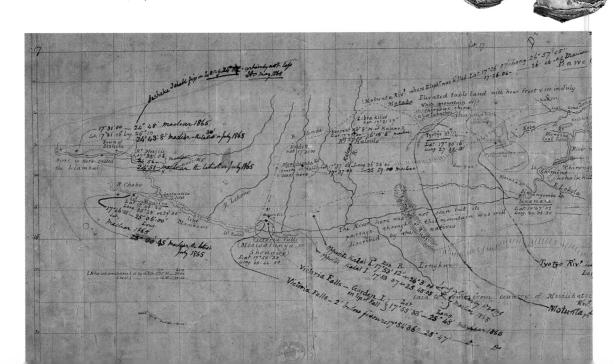

Most writers  believe the blacks to be savages, nearly all blacks believe
the whites to be cannibals. The nursery hobgoblin
of the one is black, of the other is white....
Owing to the difference of idiom, very few Europeans acquire an accurate
knowledge of African tongues unless they begin to learn when young.
A complaint as to the poverty of the language is often only a sure proof
of the scanty attainments of the complainant... A grave professor put
down in a scientific work "Kaia" as the native name of a certain lizard.
Kaia simply means "I don't know," the answer which he received.
This name was also applied in equal innocence to a range of mountains.
Every one can recall mistakes, the remembrance of which,
in after years, brings a blush to his brow.

David and Charles Livingstone, *Narrative of an Expedition to the Zambezi and Its Tributaries*, 1865.

*Though we lacked the good things of life… we possessed* salted giraffe *and pickled zebra tongues… we had sweet potatoes, tea, coffee, dampers, or slap-jacks; but I was tired of them. My enfeebled stomach, harrowed and irritated with medicinal compounds, with ipecac, colocynth, tartar-emetic, quinine, and such things, protested against the coarse food. "Oh, for a wheaten loaf!" my soul cried in agony.*
## *"Five hundred dollars for one loaf of bread!"*

*Henry Morton Stanley,* How I Found Livingstone; Travels, Adventures, and Discoveries in Central Africa; Including Four Months' Residence with Dr. Livingstone *, 1872*

exploration and, in particular, the whereabouts of David Livingstone.

Stanley was duly dispatched and, after covering a number of assignments, including the inauguration of the Suez Canal, he departed from Tanzania. Bennett had spared no expense and Stanley was well provided for.

In addition to several cartloads of equipment (six tons in all) and 160 bearers, the list of supplies included: "boats [for sailing on the lakes], rope, twine, tents, donkeys… presents for chiefs and weapons… whether for sport or defense."

### "Dr Livingstone I presume?"

In November 1871 the expedition reached "a burnished bed of silver… The Tanganyika! — Hurrah! And the men respond to the exultant cry of the Anglo-Saxon with the lungs of Stentors, and the great forests and the hills seem to share in our triumph." They pressed on to Ujiji, a small village on the borders of the lake, where, to Stanley's surprise, he was greeted in English by a man who turned out to be Livingstone's servant. Stanley's search was at an end, and the *New York Herald* had its exclusive. He walked down the street, took off his hat, and uttered those famous words that would go down in history: "Dr. Livingstone, I presume?" Livingstone had been cut off from the outside world for three years and was hungry for news.

Stanley informed him that the world had "experienced much in the last few years," including the opening of the Suez Canal and the defeat of Napoleon III's armies by the Prussians at Sedan. Then, seated around a bottle of champagne "brought on purpose for this event," the two men toasted the "happy meeting." The doctor opened some of the letters from his children brought by Stanley, and the two men "conversed upon many things."

**Above**
I took off my hat, and said: "Dr. Livingstone, I presume?"
"Yes," said he, with a kind, cordial smile, lifting his cap slightly.
I replaced my hat on my head, and he replaced his cap, and we both grasped hands. I then said aloud:
"I thank God, Doctor, I have been permitted to see you."
He answered, "I feel thankful that I am here to welcome you."
— *How I found Livingstone*, Sir Henry M. Stanley

**Opposite**
Stanley's arrival at Lake Tanganyika, one of Emile Bayard's most famous plates for *Le Tour du Monde*.

*Livingstone's body was shipped back to London, where it was formally identified from an old wound on the left shoulder, the result of* a savage mauling by a lion *in 1843.*

**Opposite**
Livingstone was a reluctant hunter and had come within inches of being mauled to death by a lion. But what he loathed most was the mosquito "of which several species show us their irritating attentions."

Stanley soon realized that there was not a grain of truth to the rumors about Livingstone, including the story of his remarriage to an "African princess."

"As to the report of his African marriage, it is unnecessary to say more than that it is untrue, and it is utterly beneath a gentleman to hint at such a thing in connection with the name of David Livingstone."

The two men found they had much in common, despite the differences in age and character (Livingstone, aged sixty, was twice Stanley's age). For Stanley, this was a major turning point in his career, a watershed between his former days as a journalist and his future life as an explorer. He would go on to make his name in equatorial Africa, and sensing perhaps the enormity of the task that lay before him, he felt a mixture of weariness and elation more intense than the stress he had felt as a reporter.

In the meantime, as leader of the *New York Herald* Expedition, Stanley's task was to bring Livingstone back alive. However, the good doctor refused to leave Africa, despite his failing health and advanced age. "To all entreaties to come home, to all the glowing temptations which home and innumerable friends offer, he returns the determined answer — No, not until my work is ended." Stanley could see it was useless to insist and after traveling a short distance together in the Great Lakes Region, the two men separated. Livingstone entrusted Stanley with his journal (taken down in shorthand by the reporter during the trip), together with letters for his children and the editor of the *Herald*, to whom he wrote the following:

"And if my disclosures regarding the terrible Ujijian slavery should lead to the suppression of the East Coast slave trade, I shall regard that as a greater matter by far than the discovery of all the Nile sources together."

**Death in the rainy season**
Livingstone persisted in his belief that the rivers Lualaba and Nile were one and the same. He didn't

live to discover that the Lualaba is in fact the first stretch of the Congo River. At the height of the rainy season, he lost his way somewhere near Lake Bangweulu, and by the spring of 1873 he was nearing his end. The entries in his posthumous journal record his decline: "18th April – Very ill at night... Took two scruple doses of quinine... 19th April – ... I am excessively weak, and but for the donkey could not move a hundred yards. It is not all pleasure this exploration." On the night of 30 April 1873, in the village of Chitambo, Livingstone died while at prayer. His African companions embalmed

**Opposite**
Livingstone's last moments in *The Last Journals of David Livingstone in Central Africa, from 1865 to His Death/ Continued by a Narrative of His Last Moments and Sufferings Obtained from his Faithful Servants Chuma and Susi* (John Murray, 1880).

*Mauch refused to believe that the natives could have been the architects of*
*the most important ruins in Africa after the pyramids.*
*Subsequently, the site of Great Zimbabwe was variously and erroneously*
*attributed to other ancient civilizations, among them a mythical, fair-skinned people*
*who were thought to be the makers of the religious artifacts found in the ruins*

one of whom was Carl Mauch (1837-1875), a German geologist who discovered a gold mine in South Africa and then led an expedition to the north of the Limpopo River. In September 1871, he found what he was looking for: a strange complex of ruins, including a huge stone enclosure and a tall, conical tower built of solid rock. He was the first European to set eyes on the ruins of the Great Zimbabwe.

The origins of the site, some two hundred miles south of Harare, remain as mysterious today as they have always been. It is estimated that the central ruins and surrounding valley supported a thriving economy based on cattle husbandry and gold mining. They are thought to have been occupied by the Shona (Bantu) population from 1100 to 1500 A.D. The word *Zimbabwe*, from which the country takes its name, means "stone houses" in Shona, but what these structures were used for — dungeons for slaves or vaults to store revenue from trade — remains unknown.

Mauch refused to believe that the Blacks could have been the architects of the most important ruins in Africa after the pyramids. He claimed that Zimbabwe was "an imitation of the temple of Solomon" and surmised that it was the site of the ancient kingdom of Saba (or Sheba). In the Old Testament (1 Kings, 10:1-13), the beautiful Queen of Sheba is said to have visited King Solomon. Subsequently, the Great Zimbabwe was variously and erroneously attributed to other ancient civilizations, among them a mythical, fair-skinned people who were thought to be the makers of the religious artifacts found in the ruins, among them a magnificent soapstone bird that later became a national symbol, incorporated into the Zimbabwean flag.

his remains with a mixture of alcohol and salt, gathered together his belongings, and carried their master to Zanzibar.

Livingstone's body was shipped back to London where it was formally identified from an old wound on the left shoulder, the result of a savage mauling by a lion in 1843. He was buried with full honors in Westminster Abbey, London. The inscription on his tombstone reads: "For thirty years his life was spent in an unwearied effort to evangelize the native races, to explore the undiscovered secrets, to abolish the desolating slave trade of Central Africa."

### The kingdom of the Queen of Sheba
Livingstone was an inspiration to countless eccentrics eager to take up a life of exploration,

### A Lake for the Archduke Rudolph

Thirty years after the Burton and Speke expedition, a wealthy Hungarian aristocrat, Count Samuel Teleki, became the first European to attempt to climb Mt. Kilimanjaro. Like Samuel Baker, Teleki was entirely self-financed and could afford to hire the services of Ludwig von Höhnel, a cartographer-cum-writer who produced an illustrated account of their travels together. Teleki never actually reached the summit of Mt. Kilimanjaro (he stopped at a point about 1,000 feet below), nor Mt. Kenya, which he also essayed, but he is remembered for his discovery, in 1888, of Lake Rudolf (named after his dear friend the Archduke of Austria,

son of Emperor Franz Joseph), in the Great Rift Valley (East Africa).

The lake was later renamed Lake Turkana after Kenyan independence. (Kenya is not the only country to have departed from the names originally chosen by 19th-century explorers. Indeed, the African Great Lakes have been renamed so many times that cartographers despair of ever getting them right.)

**Above**
Following the African Nationalist victory in 1980, the ancient ruins of the Great Zimbabwe gave their name to the present day Republic of Zimbabwe, formerly Rhodesia (an independent republic under white minority rule).

# IV

# Deep in the
# equatorial forest

In 1832, an article published in the Parisian weekly,
Revue des Deux Mondes, sparked a row that
threatened to end in disaster. The journalist responsible,
Théodore Lacordaire, accused the celebrated French
explorer Jean–Baptiste Douville of being a fraud and
an imposter who had probably never set foot in Africa.
Parisian society was appalled. Douville had recently
been awarded a gold medal by the Société de Géographie
for his book Voyage au Congo et dans
l'Intérieur de l'Afrique Equinoxiale; his
achievements had earned the recognition not only
of his peers, but of their Royal Majesties, the King
and Queen of France, Louis–Philippe and Amélie.
Douville responded in the manner of a gentleman:
by challenging the journalist to a duel.

> *"I am excessively weak, and but for*
> *the donkey could not move a hundred yards.*
> *It is not all pleasure this exploration."*
>
> Charles Livingstone

**Fortunately for both parties, the whole affair,** after a lot of commotion, eventually came to nothing. It later came to light that Lacordaire's accusations were based on an article published anonymously in the *Foreign Quarterly Review* that had been written by the British geographer William Cooley. In addition to his expertise in geography, Cooley's main specialty was running down the French: some years earlier, he had slandered René Caillié by asserting that he had never been to Timbuktu. Contemporary African specialists these days acknowledge that Douville was the victim of libel. Yet there was something vaguely suspicious about Douville. His thorough knowledge of Angola led some to suspect that he made his fortune in Brazil by trading in partnership with Brazilian slave traffickers. Despite its title, his *Voyage au Congo* is principally about Angola. (In Douville's time, "The Congo" was a term used to denote all of the regions on the river.) Regardless, Douville was an adventurer, with all the qualities of an explorer. He was an ethnographer before the term was invented; he had acquired a grounding in mineralogy while prospecting for gold for the Portuguese in Angola; and he knew a bit about botany from his observations of how the Negroes used tobacco plants "for their own personal use." He also remarked on the wealth of medicinal plants to be found in Angola. However, as he wisely pointed out in his book: "The Portuguese are not the least bit interested in anything not directly related to the slave trade. The Negroes, on the other hand, who treat everything with natural remedies, are minutely interested in their surroundings and make use of whatever Nature has to offer." Remedies used by the Douvilles ranged from quinine to "half a grain of opium to make one sleep," especially for the author's wife who always traveled with her husband and suffered from "fevers."

### The quinine revolution

In the early days of exploration, discoveries in the field of disease were almost as common as in the field of geography. For Caillié and his contemporaries, sickness was an occupational hazard and expeditions were regularly held up by the devastation of malaria. In 1827, four years after seeing his companion Dr. Oudney die, Captain Clapperton died of malaria on a return trip to Nigeria. From Anderson to Livingstone, no one was free from the scourge of malaria. Bouts of "swamp fever" came with the territory, rather like dysentery, which explorers tried to guard against by means of hygienic precautions that were often quite alien to the African carriers. Then, in 1820, two unjustly forgotten French pharmacists, Pierre Pelletier and Joseph Caventou, successfully extracted quinine from cinchona bark.

Over the course of the next thirty years, quinine became the main treatment for attacks of malaria. The final breakthrough came in 1854, when an English doctor named Baikie, on an expedition up the river Niger, demonstrated the prophylactic efficacy of quinine. It was twenty years before scientists identified that mosquitoes, and not foul "miasma," were the real cause of malaria. By that time however, Baikie's momentous discovery had opened up new horizons for explorers. It was now possible to

**Preceding double page**
"Gun boat diplomacy" was introduced by Major Faidherbe in Senegal as a show of force designed to impress African chiefs. Small, shallow-draught barges were used to move up the rivers.

**Above**
Medicine and phytogeography often go hand in hand. The caper pictured here was found to have edible buds with digestive properties.

**Opposite**
The characteristic spear-shaped leaves of the chinchinoa shrub, source of the quinine that saved many thousands of lives.

Pl. 93.

*It was now possible to plumb the* **mysteries** *of the disease-ridden swamps of equatorial Africa known infamously as the* **"white man's grave."**

venture beyond the comparative safety of western and eastern Africa, toward the disease-ridden swamps of equatorial Africa known infamously as the "white man's grave."

## The German and the Pygmy

The first European to venture to the "heart of Africa" was probably Georg Schweinfurth, a German botanist featured in countless tales of exploration. In 1868, he was commissioned by a German scientific society to conduct a three-year botanical exploration by way of Khartoum. He would eventually cross the Nile-Congo watershed, gathering unique information that would earn him the respect of his peers and establish his reputation as an African specialist for, among other contributions, providing the first authoritative account of the Congo Pygmies and cannibals.

In the Sudan, Schweinfurth had often heard the Nubians speak of dwarfs in terms that reminded him of battles in Greek mythology between the cranes and the "undersized." (The word pygmy is derived from the Greek word that denotes the distance from the elbow to the knuckle.) He also remembered that Pygmies, an endless source of fascination for Europeans, were a recurring theme in ancient Egyptian art. According to his Nubian companions, "the elusive dwarf was quite impossible to catch. He would dart beneath an elephant's belly, disembowel it with his spear, then escape, safely out of reach of the colossal trunk." Whenever Schweinfurth asked to meet the pygmies, the answer was always the same: "the little men were too shy to come to the camp." The explorer's patience was finally rewarded when a meeting was arranged with chief Adimokou of the Akka pygmies, "a small colony established half a league away." At barely four feet tall, chief Adimokou was "the tallest specimen of his kind" that Schweinfurth would ever come across. In other respects, though, the interview was a disappointment. According to Adimokou, what his people had to say was "too vague and obscure to be worth telling" and the most he was prepared to do was perform a war dance.
Eventually Schweinfurth forged good relationships with the Akkas; he and one particular pygmy even became quite inseparable, only parting when Schweinfurth returned to Germany.

## Cannibalism

Pygmies weren't the only anthropological discoveries to capture the European imagination. People also had a gruesome fascination for

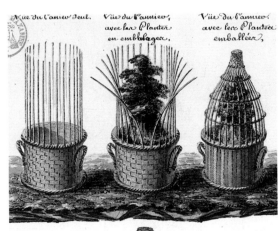

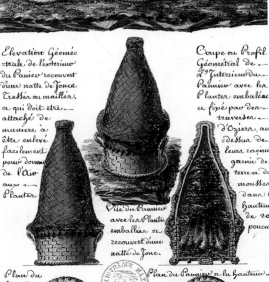

Then one morning, I heard shouting. Abd-es-Sâmate, so I discovered, was bringing me a dwarf that he had captured from the king's entourage. And there indeed was Sâmate carrying a strange little creature on his shoulder. It shook its head convulsively and looked around with panic-stricken eyes. Amâte laid his burden down on the seat of honor and the royal interpreter came forward. There before me at last was the living incarnation of a thousand-year-old myth. With no time to lose, I started to draw the creature's portrait. I had the greatest difficulty keeping it still and only succeeded by spreading out all the presents that it was shortly to receive.

Georg Schweinfurth, *The Heart Of Africa: Three Years' Travels and Adventures in the Unexplored Regions of Central Africa from 1868 to 1871*

cannibalism, which was practically an obsession in 19th-century literature on equatorial Africa. According to Schweinfurth, the most fearsome man-eaters were the members of the "Niam-Niam" tribe – whose name, by some strange linguistic coincidence, happens to rhyme with the French interjection "miam-miam," meaning "yummy." "They [the Niam-Niam] make no secret of their disgusting taste for human flesh but openly adorn themselves with necklaces made from their victims' teeth." The tribe also possessed a collection of human skulls, which they were prepared to trade for copper bracelets. "Out of the two hundred I examined, only forty were intact.... The remains had plainly been boiled and scraped with a knife; some of them were still slightly moist, suggesting that they had only recently been fished out of the stewpot."

Shortly after the Franco-Prussian war of 1870, the French explorer Alfred Marche was forced to turn back his expedition by a "very savage tribe" called the Osseybas. In his rather morbid account of the expedition, Marche deals at length with local witchcraft. "They are all fetishists," he writes of certain tribes in the Gabon and the Congo. "The only spirits they know are evil spirits to which they make offerings. Good spirits are unheard of." Marche noted how certain tribes terrorized others. "The Okandas told me that they tie a heavy stone around the necks of their dead then throw them into the deepest part of the river. It seems this is the only way to stop the Osseybas and the Adoumas from stealing the heads of dead Okandas and turning them into fetishes." So gruesome were some of the

descriptions in Marche's book that they were effectively censored by the French biannual review of exploration, *Le Tour du Monde*, which generally rather favored graphic descriptions.

## Brazza confronts the coast of Gabon

The next explorer to make his mark on equatorial Africa was the charismatic Pierre Savorgnan de Brazza (1852–1905), whom French schoolbooks describe as "the greatest French explorer of his time." Count Pietro di Brazza Savorgnani was born in Rome, the descendant of a noble Venetian family. From the age of thirteen he had set his heart on a career in the navy, which was only natural given his Venetian roots, but difficult to achieve in a newly formed republic with no established fleet. With the help of a family friend, Pietro di Brazza entered the French naval academy, later adopting French citizenship after France's defeat at Sedan. The thirst for revenge drove numbers of French

Since all the huts are small, you have to bend down to enter by the outside door and leave by the door that opens onto the village. At the foot of that door, just visible above the surface was the top of a human head. It was almost entirely buried in the earth and I was forced to step on it on my way out. A guard escorted me to where the chiefs were sitting and as we watched the men trying to catch the kid that was to be my present, I asked the chief about the head.

He paused a moment before answering, consulted one of the village elders, then to my amusement, replied that it was a gorilla's head.

"No, it's not," I laughed. "It's a human head. What's it doing there?"

The chief assured me that I was mistaken and I could see it was useless to persist. So I changed the subject but asked my interpreter to find out what he could. Once we had left the village, this is what he told me:

"It's the head of a great chief that has been stuffed with magic herbs. Any enemy who steps on it when he enters the village will surely die."

Alfred Marche, *"Voyage au Gabon et sur le fleuve Ogôoué"* (Journey to the Gabon and on the River Ogowe), 1878

*This first journey served to convince Brazza that policing the Gabonese coastline was not enough to stop the slave trade. It plainly continued to flourish despite the ban imposed by European countries.*

officers to seek adventure overseas.

Unlike most explorers, Brazza never published an account of his own. All of the chronicles of his expeditions were later published in *Le Tour du Monde*, then subsequently compiled, together with letters and lecture notes, into a single volume. One of those accounts, *Voyages dans l'Ouest African* (Travels through West Africa) begins on board the frigate Venus, bound for Gabon: "Throughout the entire crossing" admits Brazza, "my adventurous spirit raced ahead. I longed to embark on the conquest of Africa, spurred on by Livingstone's thrilling experiences. What made the prospect all the more exciting was that those spaces marked 'unknown territory' on maps of Africa appeared to be right by the coast." This first journey served to convince Brazza that policing the Gabonese coastline was not enough to stop the slave trade. It plainly continued to flourish despite the ban imposed by European countries. The following year, Brazza's plan to explore equatorial Africa in support of commerce was approved by the French Naval Minister, Admiral de Montaignac (the family friend who had previously helped Brazza to enter the Naval Academy). The plan was to sail up the Ogowe with a small entourage and enough gifts to appease the demands of hostile tribesmen. The next step was to hire carriers and pirogues and press on to the legendary Great Lakes Region—from which flow the torrents of water produced by the rain forests. The entire team consisted of twelve Senegalese sailors (known as

"laptots" in Wolof); Noël Bally, a doctor; Hamon, the quartermaster; and Alfred Marche, with whom Brazza had become acquainted. The French government had agreed to advance a year's funding.

In October 1875, the expedition reached Libreville (Congo) where the first task was to arrange transport with the locals: "not an easy task by any means with people who have never heard of money and insist on payment in kind. This means, of course, that no explorer can ever travel light." In a bid to lighten the load, Brazza introduced a daily diet based on African staple foods such as plantains and cassava.

## From frigate to pirogue

The expedition set off in convoy from Lambaréné, on the Ogooué River, site of the celebrated medical mission founded in 1913 by Albert Schweitzer. Each of the four pirogues was sixteen to nineteen feet long by barely three feet wide and made of a single piece of locally grown Okoume wood. Brazza was in the lead flying the

**Left-hand page**
Suggestive illustrations like this one contributed to the popularity of explorers' accounts. Notice the ominous skull significantly placed just a few inches from the explorer's foot: a lone white man surrounded by witch doctors.

**Above and below**
Portrait of Brazza in bush clothing (top) and in an advertisement for soap. As a precaution against dysentery, explorers washed several times a day. Félix Dubois (1862-1943), in his *La Vie au continent noir* (1893), wrote that groups of natives would gather around the tents at dawn to watch the white men at their ablutions. "They were fascinated by the white lather and obviously thought it was some mysterious substance that washed off blackness."

**Top, left and right**
Brazza's native workforce carving a canoe from a trunk of okoume (left) and portaging the canoes to avoid a waterfall (right). Scenes such as these seem to prefigure the use of "forced labor" to build the railways at the time of colonization.

**Above**
Alfred Marche, having recovered his composure.

**Opposite**
Typical representatives of tribes found in equatorial Africa.

tricolor flag and heavily loaded with supplies, including regular handouts of tobacco and rum for the Africans paddling the canoes. These men were to be paid at the end of the trip, in coupons redeemable at French trading posts.

From the moment the river entered the rainforest, Brazza saw the first signs of indigenous populations. "Lighter patches were clearly visible through the dark green foliage; everywhere I looked were plantings of cassava, pistachios, oil palms, and banana trees." On one of the first stops, Brazza made friends with the Okanda tribe, much to the annoyance of the neighboring Osseybas who had made such a nasty impression on Marche. But even the Osseybas were appeased by the French explorer, whose reassuring manner made him a born ambassador.

Brazza's descriptions of local customs are characteristic of his good-humored tolerance: "Women here have no conception of jealousy.

On the contrary, they pity any poor creature with a husband so poor that he can only afford a single wife." He can well understand how strange the white man's arrival must seem to the natives: "The brave Fans could see at a glance that we weren't cannibals but they obviously found it hard to believe that all the wonderful things we had brought with us were man-made. And when I told them that no one lacked for anything in the white man's world, they wondered why on earth we had ever left there." On one or two occasions, the temptation to demonstrate this "white man's magic" proved too much for Brazza, who put on displays of "fireworks, electrical impulses, rockets, and magnesium flares." His repeating rifle was another source of wonder, especially as the natives were convinced that it never needed reloading—an impression Brazza was careful not to contradict.

## A furious beating of war drums

Eventually Brazza was forced to abandon his initial plan to sail up the Ogooué to the Great Lakes Region. He and his men had to continue their journey on foot after reaching a waterfall where the Ogooué ceased to be navigable. They would spend the next three years exploring the dark, steamy forest with the help of local guides hired in the villages. In the end they came to another river, called the Alima by their guides, which was actually a tributary of the River Congo. Undaunted, Brazza ordered new pirogues to be built. What he did not know at the time was that he and his men had found their way into the Congo river basin.

The Alima turned out to be more treacherous than the Ogouué. Brazza and his men were now at the mercy of the Bafourous, hostile tribesmen who were strangers to white men — although apparently not to their guns. First, warning shots were fired at the pirogues. Then, one night, the air was suddenly filled with a furious beating of war drums.

Out of nowhere came a party of warriors brandishing assegais (wooden spears) and barring the river with their pirogues. Brazza was loath to use force but this time had no choice. He gave the order to fire and the tribesmen retreated as fast as they had come. However, the incident deterred Brazza, who detested violence, even when it was in self-defense. He decided to turn back on 2 August 1878. He would not make it to the River Congo — where Stanley was soon to make his name — until his return to Africa two years later.

## A "treaty" with the Makoko

News of Brazza's exploits soon spread from Libreville (capital of present-day Gabon) back to France. He returned to a hero's welcome from a public whose passion for overseas travel had acquired, with the recent prospect of colonization, a decidedly patriotic dimension. Brazza was promoted to the rank of ensign, and the Société de Géographie held a reception in his honor at the Sorbonne. Meanwhile, people in high places had plans for him. They saw in Brazza what Léopold II, King of Belgium (1865-1909), saw

**Above, left**
Brazza's convoy leaving Lambaréné. The leader of the crew, who stood at the back of the canoe, was almost as important as the interpreter.

**Above, right**
Alfred Marche capsizes in the rapids but manages to save his rifle. After an adventurous life, he would finish his career as Director of Agriculture in Tunisia.

**Above**
Brazza puts on a fine performance as a magician. He had thought to pack some old costumes that had been given to him by a Parisian theater. Velvets and silks, gold and silver braid, and costume jewelry always made a favorable impression on the Africans.

*The immense Congo, 3,000 miles long and with a basin the size of India, lay before them. From that day, it would haunt the* **French popular imagination** *just as the Nile had captivated the attentions of the British.*

in that "mercenary" Stanley: a means to an end in the conquest of Africa. France's adoptive son was to establish a French presence in the Congo region, and a new expedition was scheduled for December 1879.

By August 1880, Brazza had reached a military base in the Gabon, which he renamed Franceville because it reminded him of certain places back home. It was here that he received a messenger sent by a local king, who had heard of Brazza's interest in starting a dialogue with the Africans. More interesting still, the monarch in question happened to rule over a kingdom in the Congo. Clearly, the two men had important issues to discuss and Brazza, with a small contingent of trusted officers, agreed to follow the messenger to meet with the king. One night, after a journey made partly over land and partly by river, they spotted what looked like the sea in the distance. The immense Congo, 3,000 miles long and with a basin the size of India, lay before them. From that day, it would haunt the French popular imagination just as the Nile had captivated the attentions of the British.

In his own account of the trip, Brazza refers to the king's messenger as "Makoko." In fact, though, "Makoko" was the title of the "King of the Batekes," whom Brazza and his men visited dressed in their "finest rags." On 3 October 1880, at the end of lengthy negotiations, Brazza came away with what may be loosely called a "treaty." Laughably unfair as it was — the African signatories could neither read nor write in the language the agreement was composed in — it granted France certain "rights" over part of the Congo. In it, Brazza points out that he issued a French flag to each of the Makoko's "vassals" who signed the treaty, together with orders to "fly the flag in their respective villages as a sign that I have taken possession [of their lands] in the name of France."

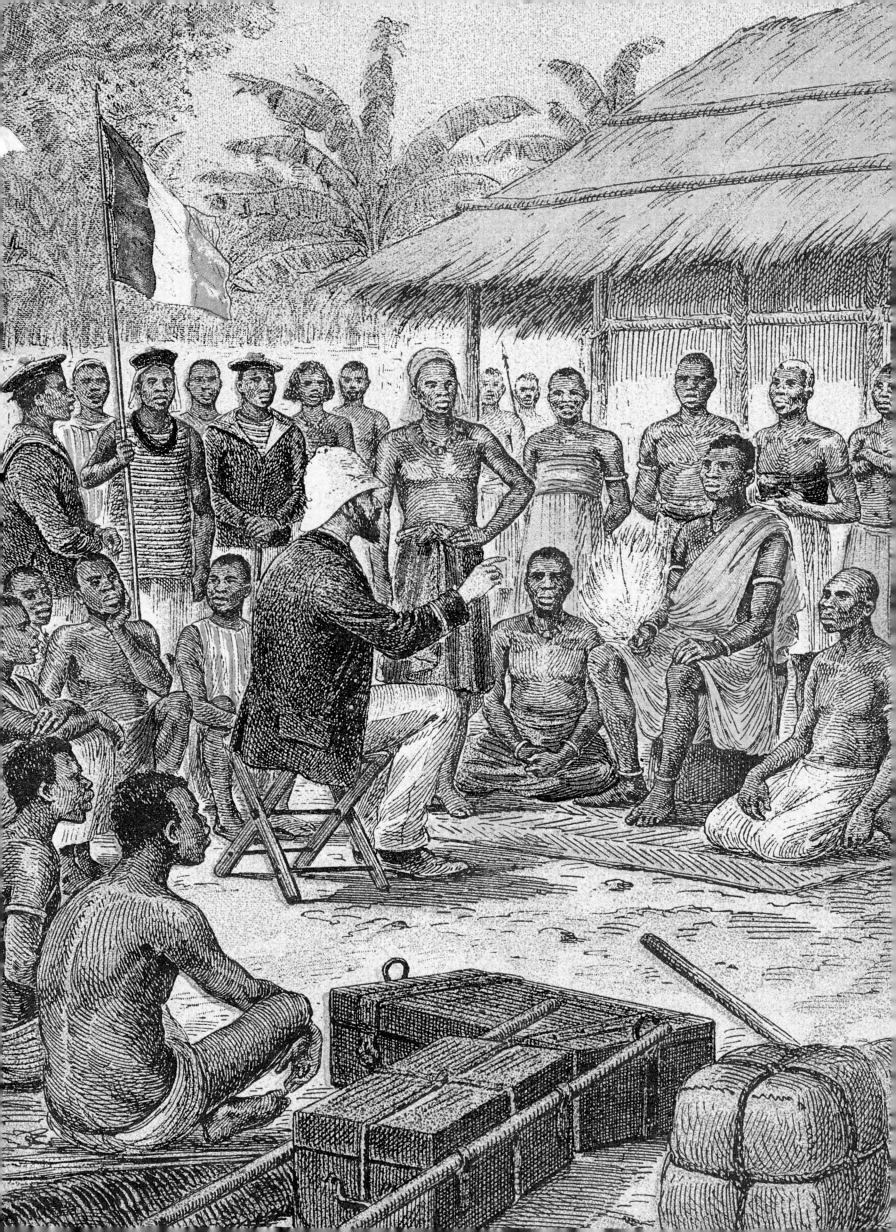

*"I issued each of the chiefs with a **French flag** that they are to fly in their respective villages as a sign that I have taken possession of their lands **in the name of France.**"*

**Preceding double page**
Stanley insisted that European trading posts on the Congo River would improve conditions for riverside communities. With just a few reasonable health measures, he thought, people living in the Congo River basin should be just as healthy as folks in the Arkansas lowlands.

**Below**
Brazza's self-control is put to the test when a local chief's daughter offers him a "dish of caterpillars."

### Brazza on the right bank, Stanley on the left

Brazza was accomplishing for the French on the right bank of the Congo River exactly what Henry Stanley was doing for the Belgians on the left bank. On his return to the Atlantic coast, Brazza crossed over to greet his rival colleague, who was not impressed. Stanley wrote in a letter that he found Brazza "unremarkable in every way except for his faded uniform, colonial frock coat, and pith helmet."

However, seven months later in February 1882, when the Welshman tried to take over the right bank, he found that the Frenchman was one step ahead of him. Before leaving the Congo, Brazza had left a Senegalese "sergeant" named Malamine in charge of defending France's latest overseas acquisition. The soldier showed Stanley a copy of the existing "treaty" between France and the Makoko and asked the Welshman to leave. When he refused, Malamine asked local chiefs to stop providing the explorer's men with food. In the end, it was hunger and not politics that drove Stanley back to the left bank. He set up camp in Kinshasha, a little village that would eventually develop into the city of Léopoldville, capital of the Belgian Congo. It later reverted to its original name in 1966 (as the capital of Zaire). Malamine was stationed directly opposite. The die had been cast: France on the right bank, Stanley's Belgian principals on the left.

Back in Paris, Malamine's courageous stand won the admiration of the Société de Géographie, which named the post he had defended "Brazzaville." Brazza was one of the few people to have a town named after them in his lifetime. The capital of the French Congo and the capital of the Belgian Congo now stood face-to-face across Stanley Pool (now Pool Malebo).

### Slaves and the French flag

Brazza was to return to the Congo several times and would even be appointed "General Commissioner" from 1887 to 1897. In 1905, missionaries in Ubangi-Shari (now the Central African Republic) raised a public outcry with reports of brutal punishment inflicted by French civil servants on their black slaves. Brazza was sent to investigate in order to set the public's mind at rest. He never returned to France alive. Officially, the cause of his death was a mysterious fever, although there was talk of poisoning. It was also insinuated that documents incriminating the colonial administration disappeared from

**Right**
Late 19th-century photograph of a white man being carried in a hammock strung between two poles. Known in Africa as a *tipoi*, it required several bearers and was only used by explorers in cases of sickness.

**Above**
All eyes turn to watch this cyclist near Brazzaville.

**Right-hand page**
Dealing with slaves once they were freed could be a problem. Brazza's solution, hiring them as paid bearers and canoe paddlers, produced very mixed results. Freedom for many slaves meant wandering all over Africa trying to get back home.

his customized, double-bottomed trunk. It had been specially made for him, as was all of his luggage, by Louis Vuitton.

Savorgnan de Brazza's mysterious death contributed to his reputation as a man of justice, a man of peaceful action who, with the exception of that one occasion on the Ogooué River when he was forced to defend himself, never opened fire on the natives. That reputation survives in Africa today. Brazzaville has retained its name, even after the Congo became independent in 1960. When the first Congolese leaders came to power they retained the colonial name without challenging the accuracy of historical accounts. Indeed, Brazza the explorer is remembered equally as Brazza the slave liberator, who pursued the agents of Zanzibar into the heart of the virgin forest.

Some would say that Brazza showed an initiative of the Gaullist type: he pursued his aims with few material means and relatively little official backing. In 1944, when General De Gaulle delivered his famous speech promising to grant independence to French colonies, it is no coincidence that he chose to give his address from Brazzaville.

## Stanley renames the African soil

After finding Livingstone, Stanley was ready to embark on a new career as an African explorer. His ambition was to explore the Congo, and thanks to his popular coverage of the Livingstone story, the *New York Herald* was prepared to finance a second expedition. The Welshman, together with a team of three hundred, departed on 12 November 1864 from Zanzibar. His heaviest item of equipment was a thirty-five-foot boat built by a carpenter from Zanzibar and delivered in kit form. Stanley named it the *Lady Alice* after his fiancée, unaware at the time that she would never become his wife. By the time he reached Boma on 8 August 1877, having crossed the whole of Africa from the Indian to the Atlantic Ocean, Alice had married another man.

This journey, like all such journeys, started with a visit to the Great Lakes Region. Shortly after the expedition headed inland, however, several of the men dropped dead from exhaustion. Then, numbers of bearers deserted after the explorer joined up with Tippo Tip, a notorious slave trader and ivory dealer from Zanzibar. A

Shortly before the Lopé market was due to close, I did as I had planned
and offered to buy any of those poor creatures waiting to be shipped to
the Lower Ogooué. But slaves are so superstitious of whites
that only eighteen of them accepted my offer. The rest preferred to remain with
their masters and depart for regions from which they would never return.

Those who came with us received a voucher to the value of
three hundred francs, redeemable at our trading posts in Lambarené,
and were then escorted to the quad at the base....
"Anyone who touches our flag," I said, pointing to the mast
where we were hoisting the colors, "is a free man because we
recognize no man's right to enslave another." No sooner had each man
touched the flag, than his neck was released from the wooden fork
and the hobble was smashed around his ankle. Meanwhile my laptots
presented arms, the flag billowing majestically in the air as if to gather
humanity's most destitute into its welcoming folds.

Savorgnan de Brazza, *Voyage dans l'Ouest African,* 1888

*His heaviest item of equipment was a thirty-five-foot boat built by a carpenter from Zanzibar and delivered in kit form. Stanley christened it the* Lady Alice *after his fiancée.*

**Above**
Stanley with his walking stick.

**Above**
Stanley with his walking stick.

**Below**
Tippo Tip's camp. Hamed Ben Mohammed (a.k.a. Tippo Tip) lost his hold over equatorial Africa when the Belgians founded the Independent State of the Congo. He retreated to Zanzibar from whence he came, where he died in 1905.

couple of years earlier, he had lent a hand to another British explorer, Verney Cameron (1844-1894), the first man to cross equatorial Africa from sea to sea in 1875. In exchange for $5,000, Tippo Tip agreed to provide Stanley with a new escort, weapons, and food.

On 5 November 1876, the expedition began again. This time, Stanley followed the upper basin of a river that he assumed — rightly, as it happens, although it was only a hunch at the time — to be the Congo. The heat was stifling and the tropical vegetation almost impenetrable. Just to add to their troubles, the men were repeatedly ambushed by local tribes mistaking them for slave hunters. Stanley did not share Brazza's aversion to violence, and by the end of the trip the order to "Fire!" had been given on thirty-two separate occasions, with casualties on both sides. Stanley often faced his opponent head-on, knowing that his whiteness always gave him the advantage of surprise: "I was saved, because my very appearance startled them."

In January 1877, having traveled several hundred miles and with the same distance still to go, the expedition came upon some spectacular falls in the Lualaba River. Stanley, no exemplar of the virtue of modesty, named them the Stanley Falls (now the Boyoma Falls, between Ubundu and Kisangani). Several hundred miles later, he applied the same approach to the naming of another celebrated site: the lake-like expansion of the lower Congo River between Brazzaville and Kinshasha that became Stanley Pool (now Pool Malebo), just as Kisangani later became Stanleyville (reverting to Kisangani in 1966).

### "To any Gentleman who speaks English at Embomma"

On 4 August 1877, Stanley reached the village of Nsanda on the right-bank of the Congo. Throughout this last leg of the journey, Stanley

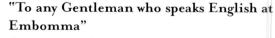

**Right**
"My position was in the bow of the boat while leading the Expedition down river .... Had I been a black man I should have long before been slain; but even in the midst of a battle, curiosity, stronger than hate or bloodthirstiness, arrested the sinewy arm which drew the bow, and delayed the flying spear... the savages became absorbed in contemplating the silent and still form of a kind of being which to them must have appeared as strange as any unreal being the traditions of their fathers had attempted to describe. *White!*"
— Stanley, *Through the Dark Continent*.

*That very evening, "by a lamp made out of a piece of rotten sheeting steeped in a little palm-butter," Stanley composed a letter* appealing for assistance.

had been unable to buy anything from the natives who "laugh at our kinds of cloth, beads, and wire." He would later write that his people were "in a state of imminent starvation" and he was at risk of having "a fearful time of it among the dying."

One night, while listening "with melancholy interest" to the headman's stories, Stanley heard there was an English merchant staying in the neighboring village of Embomma. His only hope was to write to this person "as a Christian and a gentleman… craving relief." He composed his letter that very evening, "by a lamp made out of a piece of rotten sheeting steeped in a little palm-butter." It was addressed to "any Gentleman who speaks English at Embomma" and signed "H.M. Stanley, Commanding Anglo-American Expedition for Exploration of Africa." In a postscript, Stanley added, "You may not know me by name; I therefore add, I am the person that discovered Livingston in 1871." The crucial makanda (letter) was dispatched the very next day by two of the headman's "young men," accompanied by Stanley's young assistant.

The "immediate relief" requested by Stanley did arrive, allowing him to reach the mouth of the River Congo and return to Zanzibar by boat. He then spent the next six months drafting his account of the expedition. *Through the Dark Continent*, a work in two volumes, was published to extraordinary sales in 1899.

### At the service of the King of the Belgians

Notwithstanding his success as a writer and explorer, Stanley was not popular with the British Establishment. Queen Victoria took a

dim view of his self-exposed exile to the United States and described him as an ugly, determined-looking man with a strong American accent. People in British politics did not take kindly to "stateless" people with the bad taste to fly the Stars and Stripes when they set off on expeditions. It was therefore fortunate for Stanley that his ambitious projects happened to appeal to another monarch, Léopold II of Belgium. The future founder of the Congo Free State would seriously upset the status quo in what the British described as the "scramble for Africa." This was highly unexpected: Belgium had only been recognized as an independent

**Left-hand page**
Africans from the west bank of Lake Victoria. Even Stanley commented on the good looks of certain Africans.

**Above**
Crew of the *Lady Alice*. Stanley pointed out that all the men received a new set of clothes on their return to Zanzibar. They were bound to him by individual contracts granting them monthly wages, with part of the money paid up front, the rest at the end.

**Opposite**
"The Conquest of Africa," an educational game based on Stanley and Livingstone's discoveries. Explorers also inspired highly imaginative versions of snakes and ladders.

kingdom in 1831 so as to put an end to the endless squabbles over territory in the Old World. The Belgians used to say that Léopold II "was too big a king for such a small country." He was a man of immense sexual appetites who committed indiscretions in every capital he visited. He was also a shrewd politician who, by the end of his reign, had turned his tiny kingdom into the ninth most powerful country in the world. In 1875, he attended a conference in Paris at the Société de Géographie, where Stanley and Brazza's exploits were enthusiastically discussed. The following year, he organized an event of his own in Belgium, the Geographic Conference of Brussels of 1876. Its purpose was to "bring civilization to central Africa" by establishing bases for the promotion of commerce and the exchange of geographic and ethnographic information between colonial powers. Léopold then founded the International Association for the Exploration and Civilization of Central Africa (AIA), which attracted a number of distinguished members, two of whom were the German explorer Gustav Nachtigal, who had just

made his name in Chad, and Ferdinand de Lesseps (1805-1894), who had directed construction of the Suez Canal from 1859 to 1869.

Léopold's thinly veiled imperialist ambitions soon became apparent. In 1885, knowing that Belgium was not mandated to act in a national capacity, he used his immense personal fortune to found the "Congo Free State," a private holding without precedent in the history of colonization. It occupied almost the entire

Congo River Basin and was the personal fief of the King of the Belgians. Stanley was more than willing to act as Léopold's agent, having failed to enlist support in England. Indeed, he had been called a "dreamer" for the views he expressed in the *Daily Telegraph* on 12 November 1877: "I could prove to you that the Power possessing the Congo... would absorb to itself the trade of the whole enormous basin behind."

Stanley had also said that, "without the railroad, the Congo is not worth a penny." Léopold II had taken him at his word and commissioned the Welshman to commence work on a railway that would run parallel to the non-navigable parts of the river. From 1879 to 1884 Stanley was in charge of major projects that earned him the nickname *Bula Matari* (breaker of rocks) among the natives.

### All for a few billiard balls

In 1883 alone, Henry Stanley, acting on behalf of Léopold II, finalized several hundred "treaties" with local kings, who agreed to part with their "sovereignty" in exchange for various emoluments ranging from bottles of gin to ceremonial uniforms. Gone were the days, described in *Through the Dark Continent*, of ferocious attacks by desperate men with nothing to lose; forgotten was the expedition of 1876–1877 when Stanley returned with ivory tusks worth more than $50,000 dollars. Suddenly, there were "ecological" issues to contend with: "Is it not simply incredible that, because ivory is required for ornaments or billiard games, the rich heart of Africa should be laid waste?" Within that "rich heart of Africa" there were natives in need of protection: "We see in this extraordinary increase in the number of raiders in the Upper Congo basin the fruits of the Arab policy of killing off the adult aborigines and preserving the children. The girls are distributed among the Arab, Swahili, and Manyuema harems, the boys are trained to carry arms and are exercised in the use of them." According to Stanley, who was ever anxious to promote Belgian world interests: "There is only one remedy for the wholesale devastations of African aborigines, and that is

**Above**
Stanley was in some ways an agent of European imperialism in Africa, concerned mainly with resources that would interest his Belgian masters. Other explorers focussed on the natural beauty of the continent, such as this ornithological paradise on the borders of Lake Chad.

the solemn combination of England, Germany, France, Portugal, South and East Africa, and Congo State against the introduction of gunpowder into any part of the Continent except for the use of their own agents, soldiers, and employees."

### In the days of European "pashas"

In 1885 an incident in the Nile region was to take Stanley away from his usual stamping ground in the Congo. A religious leader known as the "Mahdi" (Ahmed Ibn el Sayed Abdulla, 1843-1885) organized a revolt that overthrew the Anglo-Sudanese authority in Khartoum. The British Governor General of the Sudan, Charles Gordon, famous as "Gordon of Khartoum," was assassinated, and there were fears for the life of another government officer, Eduard Schnitzer (1840-1892), whom Gordon had appointed governor of Equatoria (in the southern Sudan) with the title of Emin Pasha in 1878. Schnitzer, a German Jew from Silesia, had converted to Islam while working as a medical officer in the Turkish Army. He was an accomplished linguist, botanist, and ornithologist who had been a consultant to all the leading museums in Europe. Following the uprising, the Egyptian government abandoned the Sudan but Emin Pasha had chosen to remain in the south, where he felt safe from whirling dervishes and political violence.

Meanwhile, the British government felt responsible for what happened in one of its former trust territories. Who better to go and rescue Emin Pasha than Henry Stanley, the man who had found Livingstone?

Léopold II quickly agreed to a new expedition, on condition that it departed from the Congo rather than Zanzibar. It was not the simplest solution, but it did allow the Belgian king to show off his African "State" to the international community.

**Above**
Ivory was not only used to make African ornaments. Demand from Europe, for the making of piano keys in particular, led to a flourishing traffic that was controlled from Zanzibar. It has been said that Africa "entered international trade" because of ivory.

**Opposite**
Elegant lady and her servant, from the Ethiopian province of Tigris. Due to distinct cultural traits that set Ethiopians apart from other Africans, their view of women was more akin to the western view. Elsewhere, young African beauties who weren't confined to Arab harems soon lost their looks through years of hard labor.

## Raining poison arrows

Stanley's new adventure began in 1887, a year that also brought new beginnings for his old friend, the former slave trader and ivory trafficker, Tippo Tip. In exchange for providing Stanley with porters, Léopold II appointed Tip "governor" of the province of Kisangani. Stanley's route would take him through hostile regions populated by warlike tribes with a reputation for archery. Showers of needle-sharp arrows rained down on the intruders, providing Stanley with quite enough samples to describe them in detail. After being baked hard in a poisoned solution: "the heads were then placed in the prepared and viscid substance, with which they were smeared; large leaves were then rolled round a sheaf before they were placed in the quiver. In a quiver there would be nearly 100

"I knew he was an ardent collector of birds and reptiles and insects, but I did not know that it was a mania with him. He would slay every bird in Africa; he would collect ugly reptiles, and every hideous insect; he would gather every skull until we should become a travelling museum and cemetery, if only carriers could be obtained.

… As long as life lasts, he will hold me in aversion, and his friends, the Felkins, the Junkers, and Schweinfurths, will listen to his querulous complaints, but they will never reflect that work in this world must not consist entirely of the storage in museums of skulls, and birds, and insects; that the continent of Africa was never meant by the all bounteous Creator to be merely a botanical reserve, or an entomological museum."

Henry M. Stanley, *In Darkest Africa, or The Quest, Rescue and Retreat of Emin, Governor of Equatoria* (1890)

*"This then, was the long promised view and the long expected exit out of the gloom," Stanley would write in November 1887 on finally emerging from the all-engulfing forest.*

arrows." The effect of the poison was slow and inexorable: "On the eighth day his neck became rigid and contracted; he could not articulate, but murmur; the head was inclined forward, the abdomen was shrunk, and on his face lines of pain and anxiety became fixed.... Morphia injections rendered him slightly somnolent; but the spasms continued, and, [he] died on the 111th hour after receiving the wound."

This was to be the last, and arguably the most testing, of the explorer's expeditions. Indeed, the word "gloom" recurs with an almost obsessive regularity throughout Stanley's account of the trip, *In Darkest Africa* (1890). The following diary entry, recorded in November 1887, when the expedition finally emerged from the all-engulfing forest, speaks volubly: "This then, was the long promised view and the long expected exit out of the gloom." The memory of that expedition — to rescue an eccentric in no hurry to return to Europe — was to haunt Stanley for many years to come.

It would take Stanley several months to convince Emin Pasha to follow him to Bagamoyo. Eventually, following disaffection among his own troops, Emin reluctantly agreed. They arrived on 4 December 1889. Back in London, Stanley received a gold medal from the Royal Geographic Society and an honorary doctorate from Oxford University. In July 1890, he married the Victorian neoclassical artist Dorothy Tenant and in 1897 he visited South Africa and wrote his account of that trip, *Through South Africa*, which was published in 1898. In 1899, he was knighted by the British, becoming Sir Henry Morton Stanley. He retired to a small private estate in Surrey (southeast England), where he died in 1904.

### Stanley's name wiped off the map of Africa

Five years before Stanley died, an English magazine published *Heart of Darkness*, a novella by Joseph Conrad excoriating the white man's role in Africa. The powerful condemnation of the treatment of the natives, which he described as "the merry dance of death and trade... in a still and earthy atmosphere as of an overheated catacomb," caused an outcry. Africa, wrote Conrad, "had become a place of darkness" with "a mighty big river... resembling an immense snake uncoiled." Nature was hostile to be sure, but that could not explain "that complete, deathlike indifference of unhappy savages." Only the Europeans were to blame for what Conrad referred to as "some sordid farce acted in front of a sinister back-cloth."

Stanley had written of his great affection for Africa and its people, while on the other hand relaying the brutal efficiency with which he fired on natives. As the radical Joseph Ki-Zerbo would write in his *Histoire de l'Afrique* in 1972: "It is the most brutal Europeans who talk the most about African hostility." A powerful commentary on Stanley's esteem in present-day Africa is that not a single place christened by him still bears his name.

**Left-hand page**
Emin Pasha deep in conversation with fellow Germans.

**Below**
Examples of the dreaded arrow heads that were shot at Stanley.

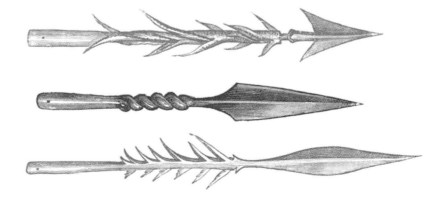

*In present-day Africa, **not a single place christened by Stanley still bears his name***

**Above**
Treasured British museum pieces: pin cushion, hat, and "leopard claws" belonging to Mary Kingsley.

**Right-hand page**
Emin Pasha's caravan in the last years of his life. Dead birds and insects were by no means his only interest. Born in Neisse in Silesian Prussia, Eduard Schnitzer (a.k.a. Emin Pasha) offered his services to the Germans after Stanley rescued him from Tanzania. Thanks to his efforts, the German influence spread throughout eastern Africa, although Pasha himself was assassinated in 1892 in the Upper Zaire. His last expedition was chronicled in a book published in Berlin in 1893 by his companion Dr Stuhlmann.

### Mary Kingsley's visiting card

Baker, Douville, and Livingstone had each taken his wife on at least one expedition, with tragic consequences in the case of Mary Livingstone. Nevertheless, 19th-century exploration remained a predominantly male domain. One exception was the British Mary Kingsley (1862-1900), niece of the clergyman Charles Kingsley, author of *The Water Babies*. Mary Kingsley was a self-taught linguist with eccentric tastes. As a child, she had devoured books on travel in her doctor father's library and set her heart on a career as an explorer. In 1893, aged thrity-one, she set sail for equatorial Africa to collect specimens of fishes for the British Museum in London. Like Brazza before her, Mary sailed up the Ogooué River with a handful of carriers and rowers. Also like Brazza, she took enough bartering "currency" — rum, fabric, bait — to obtain the specimens she wanted. Mary occasionally used the bait to catch fish herself, which she then preserved in heavy jars full of alcohol. Cups of tea were her only luxury.

Throughout the expedition, she also studied the local populations, most notably the ferocious Fang tribe in the Gabon. She was a contributor to various magazines with an enthusiastic readership by the time she published *Travels in West Africa* (Macmillan, 1897). The book sold well even though its title was misleading, considering that it was mainly about equatorial Africa.

On her return to England in 1895, Mary Kingsley became consultant to the newly appointed Secretary of State for the Colonies, Joseph Chamberlain (1836-1914). Before leaving Africa, she had climbed Mount Cameroon and wedged her visiting card between two rocks, a symbolic gesture in a dying age. For some years, England, France, and Portugal had been busy planting their respective flags in virtually every corner of Africa. The days of exploration were over. The age of colonization had arrived.

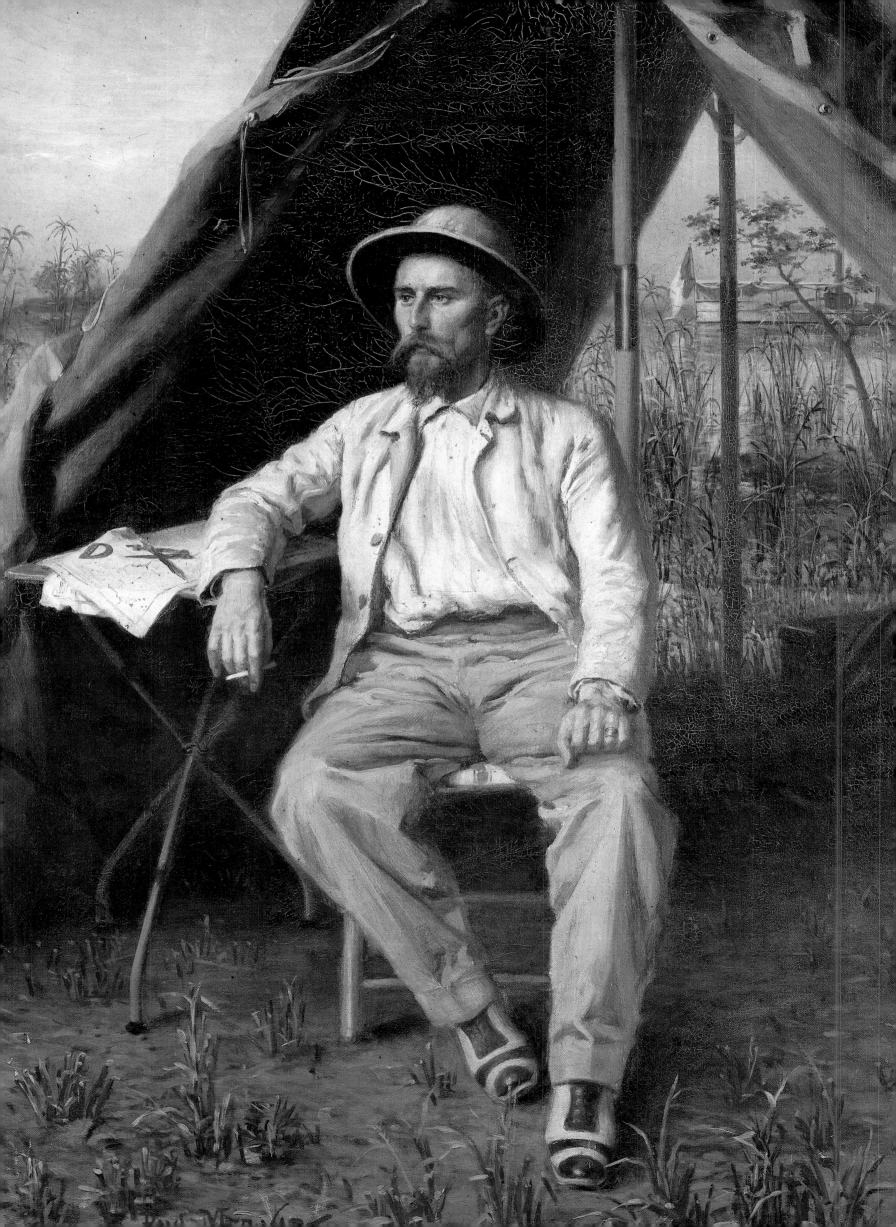

# V

# The conquerors

The town of Médine in western Mali was once dreaded on account of its torrid summers. These days, it is famous only as the place where the Bank of France hid part of its gold during the Second World War. The French fort of Médine (not to be confused with Medina in Saudi Arabia) was constructed in 1855. It was strategically positioned on the borders of Senegal and Mauritania to support French penetration of the western Sudan. The project had been masterminded by Major Louis Faidherbe (1818-1889), an army engineer officer who was to become governor of Senegal. Faidherbe collaborated closely with the Société de Géographie on "ethnographic issues relating to northern Africa." He had a genuine interest in his African subjects and was convinced that training indigenous soldiers was essential to French primacy in Africa. These recruits would eventually become known as the "Tirailleurs Sénégalais" ("Senegalese infantrymen") even though they were not all from Senegal. In 1857 there were fifty-two black soldiers garrisoned in Médine, compared with just eight Whites.

In March 1854 the holy man El-Hadj Omar (1797-1864) launched a jihad to rid his land of pagans and bring back errant Muslims. In 1857 he laid siege to the fort of Médine, which had refused to supply him with weapons. Omar had rightly calculated that the French would be unable to send reinforcements due to the low water levels on the Senegal River. What he had not bargained for was the valiant resistance put up by the French garrison. Faidherbe's gallant *Tirailleurs Sénégalais* held out until the River Senegal rose to normal levels and their commander arrived on a gunboat in person. Omar's 15,000 troops vanished. The Senegalese soldiers were decorated for bravery and every *griot* (minstrel) in Africa sang of their exploits. In France the story made the headlines, with newspapers throughout the country talking about black soldiers in fezzes waving the tricolor flag. People suddenly realized that the mysterious African could be the white man's ally against his colored brothers.

### Under French protectorate

The French troops sent out to Africa in the early days were marines who served as the infantry. They were known as "La Coloniale" (colonial regiment) and consisted of a few hundred men scattered throughout the region. Despite their initial successes, they knew themselves to be vastly outnumbered by thousands of unpredictable natives ready to attack at the slightest provocation. Seduction, rather than confrontation, was required here. Captain Joseph Galieni (1849-1916), who was later to become governor of the French Sudan, was in favor of protectorate "treaties." He set about winning privileges for France in the Upper Niger region. In exchange for freedom of passage and freedom to trade, the French agreed to recognize the "sovereignty" of local chiefs. In other words, they promised to back the chiefs in the event of vassal uprisings, which were fairly common at the time, as most societies in Africa were feudal.

The first of these treaties was signed in 1880 with the Amir Ahmadou, eldest son of Omar, who had attacked the fort of Médine some twenty years earlier. Gallieni's accounts of the negotiations, which were initially signed "Commander Gallieni of the Marine Infantry," were later published in *Le Tour du Monde*. With some tongue in cheek, Gallieni would comment on "the absurd airs and graces of Negro princes in these parts" and the fierce rivalries "between all these kings and kinglets lording it by the dozen in miserable villages round these parts." Ahmadou would later renege on the treaty of 1880 and rebel against French rule. However, his grandson would find favor in the eyes of Gallieni's successor General Louis Archinard (1850-1932), so much so that the young man was eventually accepted by the prestigious French military academy of Saint Cyr — Gallieni's alma mater.

### Saving souls

French military authorities respected the Muslim religion of the Senegalese soldiers. In the 20th century, they would acquire their own specially built mosque in Fréjus, the town in the south of France where they were trained.

**Above, right**
The *Tirailleurs Sénégalais* (right-hand page) were not the only objects of Faidherbe's affections. Beneath that austere appearance was a man who fell in love with a beautiful young African woman, moved her into the Governor's Palace, and fathered her child.

**Above**
Joseph Gallieni (1849-1916), the star of the Marine corps, served in Black Africa, Tonking, and Madagascar. He then became Minister of War in 1915, two years after retiring from the army.

**Preceding double page**
Portrait of a complete man: the casual but chic sailor-turned-explorer Emile Gentil (1866-1914). After accompanying Brazza on his travels through equatorial Africa, he struck off alone to the Upper Chari as far as Lake Chad where he studied the region's natural resources.

**Opposite**
Queen Victoria holds out a
Bible to an African, in this
large painting by Thomas
Jones Barker (1813–1882)
titled *The Secret of England's
Greatness*. In the 19th century,
the "conversion" of
indigenous populations
to Protestantism or
Catholicism depended on
the dominant European
power in their part of Africa.

However, many people thought that converting local populations to Roman Catholicism offered the best chance of peace. Animist cultures were a particular target, being less "evolved" and more malleable than those of Islam. Did these "savages" have souls? Missionaries thought that they did. Whatever Livingstone's initial setbacks, the discovery of the Zambezi River basin by the British had led to the spread of Protestantism. France's discovery of the Senegal and Congo River basins would produce a similar effect, with the arrival of three Catholic orders "specializing" in Africa. They were the Holy Spirit Congregation in Paris (Spiritains); the Society of African Missions (SMA) from Lyon; and the Society of African Missions (White Fathers).

In fact, Spiritains had been active for many years in some of the oldest French colonies, such as Canada, the West Indies, and Pondicherry (southeast India). In 1778, two members of the order had set sail for Guyana but subsequently were taken prisoner by Moors in Mauritania.

After their release, they went on to discover Senegal, where the whole of Africa, it seemed, lay waiting to be converted. They then merged with the Society of the Sacred Heart that was working to improve conditions for the victims of slavery. Meanwhile, the Society of African Missions was founded in 1856 in Lyon, France, by Melchior de Marion Bresillac (1813-1859). After serving nine years as a missionary in India he set sail for Africa in 1859 but died five weeks later of yellow fever. These pioneering missionaries established trading posts at military bases throughout the Gulf of Guinea, but they were soon to encounter competition from Protestants in Sierra Leone.

### White Fathers from Algiers to Tanganyika

The Society known as the "Pères Blancs" or "White Fathers" was founded by Cardinal Charles Lavigerie (1825-1892) in 1868. Its name derives from the white cassock that is still worn by the missionaries, not as protection from the sun but in honor of heir founder's wishes. He believed

that missionaries should dress in white robes very like the traditional *gandoura* worn by North African men. On arrival in Algiers, Lavigerie had dreamed of converting the local populations and began by spreading the word among the Berbers. However, the French authorities soon put a stop to his activities, pointing out that stealing souls from Mohammed was not in the interests of peaceful colonization. In 1868, Lavigerie was authorized by the Holy See to establish "a prefecture apostolic of the western Sahara and the Sudan, or Land of the Negroes," from which to preach and gather souls.

In 1875, three of Lavigerie's missionaries departed for Timbuktu, forty-seven years after René Caillié became the first European to set foot there. Their aim was to buy up young Negroes destined to be sold as slaves and then send them forth to preach in the Sudan. That aim was never to be fulfilled — all three missionaries were massacred by their guides.

Today the White Fathers, the Spiritans, and the SMA are international denominations welcoming members from all over Europe (alongside an increasing proportion from Africa). Nationality is irrelevant. This was not always the case. Léopold II once offered to fund a mission on his territory in the Congo on condition that it would be run by the Belgian Fathers. Cardinal Lavigerie refused out of national pride, preferring to send his men to the African Great Lakes Region, notably Tanganyika. The enemy was no longer Islam, but the British and the Germans. Missions were usually based some distance from early colonial administrative

**Above**
Traveling missionaries in Angola.

**Below**
Charles Lavigerie (1825-1892), founder of the White Fathers.

*The ferocious debate* between the religious and secular worlds that divided 19th-century France was entirely forgotten in Black Africa.

buildings, to keep the Church distinct from the State in the minds of local people. The two did however often have interests in common. The ferocious debate between the religious and secular worlds that divided 19th-century France was entirely forgotten in Africa. In his book on the discovery of western Africa, *Du Niger au Golfe de Guinée* (1892), the French explorer Louis-Gustave Binger would end with a rousing call for colonization based on four cardinal principles. They were: "the building of wharves"; "the organization of postal services"; "the opening of schools"; and the "provision of facilities for our brave missionaries."

African mores, especially sexual mores, were plainly as alien to the missionaries as their own celibacy was to the Africans. Most missionaries nevertheless made a real effort to understand their flock, producing the earliest ethnological data available on Africa. Many of them learned the local languages and published works that soon became benchmarks in the study of African dialects. Missionaries continue to write some of the best English-Swahili and French-Wolof dictionaries available.

### Serpa Pinto's heroic self-restraint

The Portuguese had been the first to take the Word of God to Africa in 1428 when they reached the mouth of the River Congo. By the late 1800s, largely due to Livingstone and the efforts of Protestants in general, they had come to be seen as former slavers who had no right to preach Christian charity to their erstwhile African victims. Meanwhile, the growth of the British and French missions in Africa was resented by the Portuguese who also objected to the "Protectorate" policies applied by the British and French governments. In Lisbon these were considered violations of former ancient "rights" that were rooted in "treaties" concluded with the first Portuguese navigators.

The capital of the Portuguese province of Mozambique remained located on the tiny coral island of Maputo, half a mile from the mainland and slightly more than one square mile in area. It was here that Saint François-Xavier had spent six months on his way to the Indies in 1541 and met the very first African converts, the Makonde people. Their carved wooden masks representing Christ on the Cross are still much sought-after

Become a Negro amongst Negroes to judge them as they should be judged. Become a Negro amongst Negroes to teach them as they should be taught. Not as Europe would want them taught, but leaving their birthright intact. Become used to them as servants become used to their masters. All this to perfect and sanctify them, lift them up from their baseness and little by little, with time, turn them into God's people.

Taken from the teachings of R.P. Libermann,
founder of the Fathers of the Immaculate Heart of Mary, 1842.

today. The tiny city of Maputo was home to no fewer than six chapels devoted to a variety of saints and martyrs. The impressive Governor's Palace of Saint-Paul was built entirely of the ochre-colored stone shipped from Portugal in the 16th century by huge convoys of caravels. On the other side of Africa, Luanda was the largest city on the west coast, with a white population of more than 1,000 people by the early 1880s.

When Portuguese officer and explorer Major Alexander Serpa Pinto crossed the African continent from west to east in 1877-1879, it was mainly to discourage the British from colonizing the Zambezi basin. With that in mind, Pinto would emphasize the "continuity" of Portuguese Africa that stretched from Mozambique to Angola. He would also highlight the favorable match between the Angola and Mozambique economies. Although his eminently political mission did not bring the anticipated results, it remains famous in Portugal as one of the most

colorful travel accounts ever written. Pinto describes how, night after night, he would dazzle prowling lions with magnesium flares and shoot them while they were immobile. In another famous passage, he explores the recurring theme of sexual relations between white explorers and African women. "My decision to remain celibate had given me enormous authority over my Negro men. Having committed no sexual indiscretions, I was regarded as a man unfettered by human frailties." However, after causing offence by initially declining the offer of a night with the local chief's daughters, Pinto was forced to think again. The girls had been offered as a token of their father's hospitality, and it would have been ungracious to refuse. To prove that he did not,

*In 1883, Edward Lüderitz, an adventurer from Bremen,*
*planted the* **German flag** *on a piece of land made up*
*of various plots purchased from Khoikhoi chiefs*

as the chief suggested, prefer Portuguese women, Pinto ended up in a cozy tête-à-tête with two charming girls reclining on leopard skins. By the light of the fire, he admired "the innocent features and naked breast of a young, sixteen-year-old woman, who gazed at me longingly with eyes full of promise. As the raucous, savage music gradually faded outside, I watched her heaving, majestic bosom, unable to tear my eyes away from her naked breasts." Similar situations were described by other explorers, then later by colonial administrators. But neither they nor Pinto ever say what happened in the end.

### Bismarck changes his mind

When Prince Otto von Bismark (1815-1898) became leader of a newly united Germany, he did not intend to squander his country's energies in Africa. "The colonies," he said in 1870, "would be to us the Germans what silk-lined sable coats are to the Polish aristocracy, who have no shirts to wear underneath." Accounts of exploration were nevertheless all the rage in Berlin, and there were by now some distinguished German explorers. What's more, they had political views. Schweinfurth, who discovered the Pygmies, wrote in his book, *In the Heart of Africa,* that the "excessive fragmentation of the African peoples" was the "main obstacle standing between them and civilization." Elsewhere he recommended the "founding of great Negro states under European protectorates" as a means of combating the illegal slave trade to Zanzibar. Germany was increasingly called upon to join the colonial adventure, not only by the periodical *Kolonialzeitung,* but also by geographical

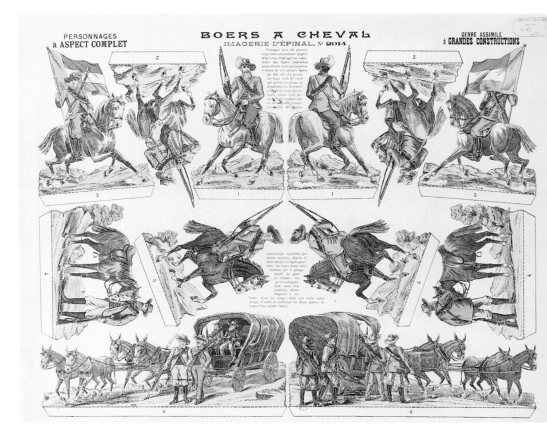

associations and commercial groups, especially those in Hanseatic towns. Germany was faced with an "existential choice," said German academics. Bismarck, being a pragmatic man, decided that colonization might not be such a bad idea after all, especially when it came to winning votes. In a dramatic about-face typical of a man who never did things by halves, Bismarck changed his mind and fully expected his diplomats and explorers to do the same.

**Above**
Cutouts of Boers, on horseback, who were not professional soldiers but experienced hunters and therefore able marksmen. Paper cutouts like these became extremely popular after the second Boer War (1899-1902), when Dutch colonists in the Orange Free State and Transvaal declared war on Britain. In the first Boer War (1880-1881), the Boers sought to regain the independence they had exchanged for British aid against the Zulus.

*At the center of the debate were the* **Rivers Niger** *and* **Congo** *that had been a focus of exploration from the start.*

## Exotic fertilizers

For many years, German missionaries had been trying to convert the people of South West Africa (present-day Namibia). So far, the nomadic Herero tribesmen had resisted all offers of Godliness, much preferring libations to devotions. Wines and spirits were shipped in by Europeans, in exchange for the region's only valuable commodity: guano or bird droppings. The islands all along the coast were home to thousands of nesting birds, whose excrement was an excellent fertilizer. In 1883, Edward Lüderitz, an adventurer from Bremen, planted the German flag on a piece of land made up of various plots purchased from Khoikhoi chiefs. The British, alerted by its colony in the Cape, warned the Germans that it had "rights" in the region. Bismarck replied that Lüderitz was acting with the Reich's backing under German protection. The young man from Bremen then calmly founded the German Society for the Colonization of South West Africa, before dying quite suddenly in 1885. He was succeeded by a certain Dr Göring, father of Reichsmarschall Hermann Göring, Commander in Chief of the German Luftwaffe. London backed down and Bismarck moved his pawns elsewhere, first to west Africa, then to Tanganyika. In 1870-1874, the German explorer Gustave Nachtigal (1834-1885) had conducted a scientific expedition across the Sahara. His account of the trip, *Sahara und Sudan*, secured him a worldwide reputation as a serious writer. Léopold II quickly saw a use for Nachtigal's mapping abilities in the Congo and made him a member of the International African Association. Some time later, Nachtigal traded the thrills of discovery for

**Top, right**
Portrait of Gustav Nachtigal, the German who upset Paris when he sailed from Togo to the Cameroon (which was coveted by the French) and signed a protectorate treaty on 14 July 1884 (Bastille Day, the French public holiday that commemorates the start of the French Revolution). The French Third Republic was not impressed.

**Above**
Nachtigal's ship.

the comforts of life as a diplomat, following his appointment as German Consul in Tunis. He was then asked by Bismarck to leave for the west coast of Africa on the warship *Mowe* (The Seagull). It was supposed to be a business trip but Nachtigal's real brief was to carve Germany another slice of Africa.

Having reached the African coastline, he sailed from the Atlantic coast to the Gulf of Guinea in a canoe and landed on the golden sands of present-day Togo. In July 1884, following successful negotiations with the indigenous populations, Nachtigal declared Togoland to be a German protectorate (*schutzgebiet*). He then signed similar agreements with the people of Cameroon, before dying in the Gulf of Guinea in 1885.

## The Congo, "Danube of Africa"

It was plain to Bismarck that bilateral treaties agreed between explorers and local chieftains required international recognition. With that in mind, he convened the Berlin West Africa Conference, a diplomatic marathon lasting from 15 November 1884 to 26 February 1885. All the major players were there — Germany, France, Britain, Belgium, and Portugal — together with more minor European colonial powers. Ambassadors were also invited from the United States and the Ottoman Empire "to ensure general approval for the conference resolutions." Stanley also came, officially with the American delegation but mainly to pursue the interests of Léopold II.

At the center of the debate were the Rivers Niger and Congo, which had been a focus of exploration from the start. Bismarck described the Congo as the "Danube of Africa" and called for both rivers to be put under international control. He wanted freedom for trade and shipping for all states in the Congo River basin (which would become a free-trade zone). Like so many international conferences, this one ended in a series of vague compromises. The great "slicing up of the African cake" did not happen,

**Above**
Zanzibar in 1886. For years, the island and its port represented everything that white men found exotic about Africa. After slavery was declared illegal by the Conference of Berlin, all the slave ships were destroyed.

**Following double page**
Inauguration of the Suez Canal.

because too many ulterior motives got in the way. Having failed to agree on the essentials, the major powers added the question of African rights to the agenda. The conference declaration included an "explicit guarantee" of "freedom of conscience and religious tolerance" towards the Africans, plus "the right of nationals and foreigners to erect religious buildings." Much to the delight of the missionaries, it also recognized "the right to establish missions of various denominations." The slave trade was declared illegal for the umpteenth time. England proposed a ban on the sale of alcoholic beverages but Germany, anxious to protect its sales of beer to Black Africa, objected in the name of free trade.

### Birth of Eritrea

Spain and Italy also put in an appearance at the conference, although neither was directly involved with Africa at the time. Spain mainly had designs on Latin America; and Italy, so soon after reunification (1861), had no experience of either exploration or colonization. Nevertheless, in 1869, an Italian missionary acting for the Rubattino Shipping Company in Genoa had "bought" Port Assab (in present-day Eritrea)

from local sultans. Such sales were possible at the time in regions under no central control. Assab was chosen with the prospect of making lucrative profits following the opening of the Suez Canal at the end of that year. Following the conquest of Rome in 1870, the Italian government "bought back" Assab in 1882 as the jumping-off point for the country's first African colony, Eritrea. Five years later, the sultan of Zanzibar agreed that part of the coastal area in present-day Somalia should become an Italian-controlled protectorate. In 1892, Captain Vittorio Bottego (1860-1897) departed from Berbera, destined to become the first person to explore the Massaua-Assab coastline. After exploring inland Somalia and parts of Ethiopia, he died in an ambush on the return trip in 1897.

### The Negus' resistance

Italy, now established in the Horn of Africa, set its sights on Ethiopia. Various characteristics distinguished this landlocked country from Black Africa in the strict sense of the term. It had its own official language, Amharic, thanks to which most people were broadly familiar with its long and eventful history. It had its own

**Above**
Battle of Dogali (Eritrea), 1887, Italy's first defeat at the hands of Ethiopian troops commanded by Ras Alula, lieutenant of Emperor Johannes IV. The word "ras" ("head of battle" or "field marshal" in the Horn of Africa) was first coined by European newspapers at the end of the 1880s.

*The Ethiopians obtained **backing** and **weapons**, and they were ready for the Italians when they marched on Ethiopia*

doctrine, Monophysitism, condemned by the Council of Chalcedon in A.D.451 but still the basis of Ethiopian Christianity. It had powerful dynasties with legendary names dating back to the time of the Queen of Sheba, mother of Menelik I.

On 2 May 1889, the Italians signed a treaty with Menelik II (1844-1913) granting them rule over Eritrea. But Ethiopia was no mere African fief and Menelik was certainly no kinglet. This time the treaty was written not only in the white man's language but also in Amharic, which would soon lead to conflict. In the Italian text, Rome was the medium for all of Ethiopia's foreign relations. The Amharic version, by contrast, was noncommittal.

The Negus (title of the emperor of Ethiopia) immediately moved into action. Since the opening of the Suez Canal, he had been surrounded by an army of foreigners, diplomats, ambassadors, and other Europeans with designs on the region. He now obtained foreign backing and weapons, and he was ready for the Italians when they marched on Ethiopia from Eritrea. Menelik's troops, commanded by Makkonen, father of future emperor Haile Selassie, proved more than a match for the 18,000-strong Italian contingent (of whom only 8,000 were actually Italians). On 1 March 1896, Italian lines crumbled at the celebrated Battle of Adawa, the decisive Ethiopian victory that put a stop to Italy's empire-building ambitions in Africa. Ethiopia still stands as the only African country never to have been colonized. Addis Ababa became a symbol of African nationalism, even though it remained quite feudal compared with the western-style cities founded elsewhere by whites. In 1963, as country after country acquired its independence, Addis Ababa became the chosen seat of the Organization of African Unity.

## Kitchener crushes the dervishes

The Sudan derives its name from the Arabic *bilad as-Sudan* ("Land of the Blacks") which was the term used by medieval Arab geographers. In the 19th century, this vast tract of land extending between the Sahara and the equatorial rain forest was divided into French Sudan (now Mali) and Egyptian Sudan (present-day Sudan). The latter was conquered by Mehemet Ali of Egypt in 1820, then made an Anglo-Egyptian condominium in

**Above**
Menelik II, who succeeded Johannes IV, took advantage of the rivalry between whites to expand his kingdom. In the course of his long reign (1889-1913), Ethiopia became a centralized modern state, with European powers vying for the king's favors after Ethiopia's victory over the Italians. French cultural influence spread among the Ethiopian elite after the signing of a treaty of friendship with France in 1897. Just as the word "ras" had come to replace "general" in the context of Ethiopia, so "Negus" ("king of kings" in Amharic) became the accepted European term for an Ethiopian emperor.

*The two men had met at the inauguration of the Suez Canal. Baker himself had been invited by another celebrated guest, the Prince of Wales, who had asked the explorer to organize* **a crocodile hunt.**

1899. The British were especially active in the southern, Equatorial Province. The Governor was none other than Sir Samuel White Baker, the distinguished British explorer who had discovered Lake Albert in 1864. He was on good terms with Mehemet Ali's grandson Ismail Pasha (1830-1895), the viceroy and khedive of Egypt, whom he had met at the inauguration of the Suez Canal. Baker himself had been invited by another celebrated guest, the Prince of Wales, who had asked the explorer to organize a crocodile hunt. One of Baker's nieces was to become the young wife of another distinguished figure, Field Marshal Sir Horatio Herbert Kitchener (1850-1916).

The Egyptian Sudan had captured the imagination of the British public. It was to become famous for such outstanding statesmen as the flamboyant Charles Gordon (1833-1885), otherwise known as "Gordon Pasha" or "Gordon of Khartoum," who succeeded Baker as governor of Equatorial province, later becoming governor general of the country as a whole in 1877. News of his assassination by Islamic Mahdist forces in 1885 (from the Arabic *mahda*, to guide aright) gave rise to widespread grief in England. After taking Khartoum on 26 January 1885, the dervishes (the name given by Europeans to the Mahdi's black Muslim followers) decapitated Gordon on the steps of his palace. They then presented his head to their leader, before jamming it between the branches of a tree — where it was stoned and reduced to a pulp. It was thirteen years before Queen Victoria would reap her revenge, when the dervishes were crushed by Lord Kitchener's forces at the Battle of Omdurman, on 2 September 1898. Kitchener's entry into Khartoum as commander in chief of the Anglo-Egyptian army crowned a campaign that had been covered by all the leading war correspondents. One of them was the future British Prime Minister, Sir Winston Churchill (1874-1956), then a journalist with a London newspaper.

### White man's war in Fashoda

The British believed that the only way to hold onto Egypt was to control the Nile from end to end. The Sudan was a vital part of that strategy. The French meanwhile felt that Egypt belonged to them and regarded the British as usurpers. The recent construction of the Suez Canal, directed by the French diplomat Ferdinand Lesseps, was tangible proof of an involvement that had started with Napoleon Bonaparte in 1798. To fulfill France's expansionist ambitions, in February 1896 the French Government instructed Captain Jean-Baptiste Marchand (1863-1934) to lead an expedition to the Upper Nile and occupy Fashoda (Sudan). His official orders were to explore unknown regions in southern Sudan to see whether they provided "a natural extension of French possessions in

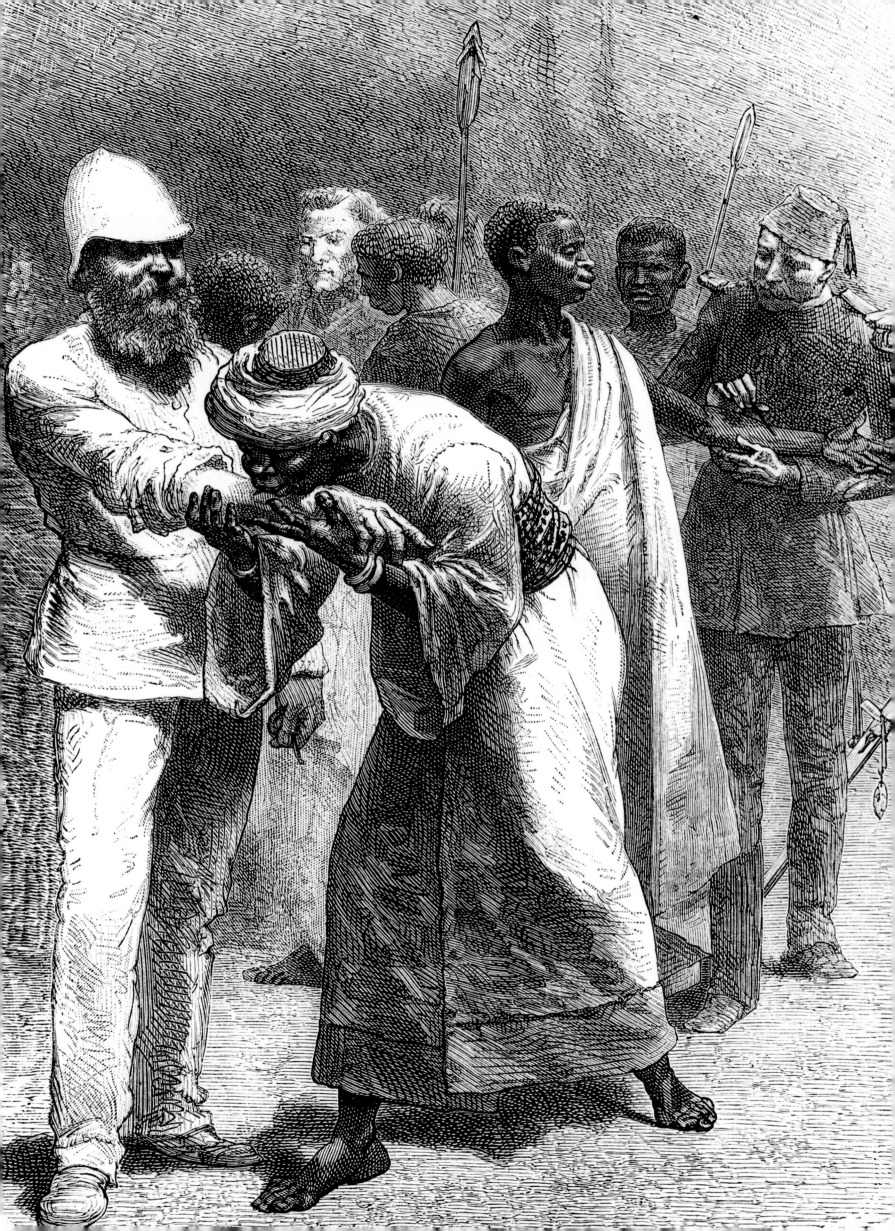

*Neither the French nor the British were prepared to go to war over Africa, where they were already hard pressed to subdue native insurrections.*

central Africa." Unofficially, he was to reach amicable agreements with local monarchs who favored French interests.

The Marchand Mission, consisting of ten French officers and a force of 150 Senegalese *tirailleurs*, departed from Brazzaville (French Congo) in January 1897. A doctor, an interpreter, and a "landscaper" (who soon turned back) had also been recruited. Vital provisions aimed at buying the support of the African chiefs included some 65,000 yards of fabric and sixteen tons of glass beads, in addition to 1,300 bottles of claret, plus champagne, cognac, and various other delicacies.

After steaming up part of the Congo, then switching to pirogues on the Oubangui, the expedition came to a succession of lesser rivers, some more manageable than others. Then Marchand's packable steamer, the *Faidherbe*, ran aground in a Nile tributary, and from that point, progress was painfully slow. On 30 June 1898, the Marchand Mission reached the banks of the White Nile and on 10 July they arrived in Fashoda (Sudan). Augustin Baratier, Marchand's companion, described the region as a once prosperous area now "ravaged by dervishes and weather." Only the battlements and the fort overlooking the Nile were still standing. Undaunted, a triumphant Marchand raised the French flag, convinced that he would win the hearts of the local people just as Brazza had done in the Congo.

London immediately protested against what it described as a policy of "fait accompli." Kitchener, having learned of the occupation of

Fashoda from captured Mahdists, left Khartoum on 10 September with four gunboats carrying British (Scots) and Sudanese soldiers. On 19 September, having sailed nearly 400 miles upstream and battled against violent tropical storms, Kitchener and his troops landed at Fashoda. He then sent a letter announcing his arrival to Marchand. The irony of the story is that Kitchener was a French-speaking Francophile. His distinguished performance alongside Napoleonic troops in the Franco-Prussian war of 1870 had earned him a French military decoration. His meeting with Captain Marchand was a model of "military correctness" and good form. It was covered by a special correspondent from the British *Daily Telegraph* and all the social niceties were properly observed. But not even champagne and whiskey could disguise the nature of Kitchener's demands. "I at once stated that the presence of a French force at Fashoda and in the Valley of the Nile was regarded as a direct infringement of the rights of the Egyptian government and Great Britain, and I protested in the strongest terms against their occupation of Fashoda and their hoisting the French flag in the dominions of His Highness the Khedive."

Kitchener knew that France was in no position to resist. To make his point, he showed Marchand a selection of the latest Parisian newspapers, freshly arrived from Cairo. They were all talking about the Dreyfus affair and how it was dividing the government and the military. Marchand realized the hopelessness of the situation and agreed to remove his troops. For

*Binger first learned Bambara, then Wolof, in the months he spent*
## planning the railway link *between Kayes and Bamako.*

**Above**
Equestrian portrait of Jean-Baptiste Marchand (1863-1934), a French hero
who was as famous in France as Gordon was in Great Britain.

**Right and following page**
Marchand occupied a special place in the long list of soldiers who were
"beaten due to civilian mistakes." His adventures were glorified in French
popular imagery and the illustrated press. He is seen here in two cover
illustrations for the *Petit Journal*, advancing through the jungle and the desert.

the sake of national self-respect, the Marchand Mission did not turn back but pressed on to Djibouti, where it arrived six months later. With British permission, Marchand then contacted the French community in Cairo and gave a stirring address describing the French humiliation and hinting at revenge. "The granite Sphinx as it dreams in the sands of Lesseps' noble enterprise has yet to say its final word, has yet to pass ultimate judgement." On his return to France, Marchand became the idol of the French nation, renowned as much for his valor as for his patriotic eloquence. But neither the French nor the British were prepared to go to war over Africa, where they were already hard pressed to subdue native insurrections.

### The crafty Commander Binger
Officer-explorer Louis-Gustave Binger (1856-1936) was just a young lieutenant when he led various scientific missions to Senegal and the French Sudan. In 1893, following further explorations of the Niger meander and the interior of the Ivory Coast, he became the first governor of the French Ivory Coast colony. The colonial capital on the borders of the Abidjan Lagoon was named after him in his lifetime and remains so to this day. In his memoirs, Binger would write that it was "because Caillié could pass himself off as a Muslim that he failed to secure any treaties. Better by far to remain exactly what one is. To advance without denying one's religion or nationality displays a strength and daring that can only inspire respect among the Blacks." Binger certainly had no lack of daring.

In 1888, he and his colleague Marcel Treich-Laplène were the first Europeans without a military escort to enter the mysterious city of Kong, deep in the Ivory Coast savanna. Binger was always prepared to speak his mind, sometimes fruitlessly, and protested against barbaric customs such as the amputation of the hands of thieves. He personally attended such amputations. In his memoirs, Binger would describe his tactics when advancing in hostile terrain. He would turn up in the villages on market day, when the mere sight of a white man was sure to draw large crowds. He would then distribute little favors and leave it to his skilful interpreters to get people to talk, especially about the local chief. Then, properly briefed, Binger would use his newly acquired knowledge to ingratiate himself with the chief. Eventually Binger was able to do without the interpreters, having first learned Bambara, then Wolof, in the months he spent planning the railway link between Kayes and Bamako.

## An African Vercingetorix

A year before his entry into Kong in 1887, Binger had made the acquaintance of Samory Touré, a Muslim leader "born circa 1830" in the north of present-day Guinea. He ruled over an "empire" in the Upper Niger and was known at the time as an Almany, a Malinke term for "political chief" and "spiritual leader." He was in fact a warrior leader, described by African schoolbooks as "our Vercingetorix." But what Binger found most striking about Touré was the number of wives he owned: "One would suppose that he would choose only the most beautiful women. Far from it, there were few pretty women among those I saw. He takes some with him everywhere just to show how many he owns — probably around a hundred or so." The little gifts with which Binger thanked the ladies for their hospitality made a significant dent in his resources. "Here is a detailed list of what I sent them: 12 coral necklaces with gold clasp; one

*Over the years, these "Amazons" had come to include maidens not yet deflowered by the king but his to dispose of as he pleased.*

**Above**
Binger negotiating with Samory inside his camp. This is how Binger described his African calling in *Du Niger au golfe de Guinée*: "As an officer in the Marine infantry I could hardly have remained indifferent at a time when all the major powers in Europe were rushing into Africa. That was where I wanted to go: to the heart of that great unknown."

length of lace; one roll of fabric; and, on request, six razors to be used as required."

Binger's attentions were largely lost on Samory, who, shortly after their meeting, declared war on the French. Samory then spent the next two years holding out against the French colonel Louis Archinard (1850-1932), alternating ambushes with the pretense of negotiations. Then in March 1891, before Samory had time to rally the most militant Muslim tribes, the French marched on his kingdom of Bissandougou, in Guinea. This was, however, no battle of Adowa, and the numbers involved were significantly smaller: 800 Muslims against sixty-three Europeans. In fact, Samory's resistance was as inadequate as it was short-lived. Archinard would later write that all the wonderful stories about Bissandougou were a myth. "The famous metropolis" turned out to be no more than an African village — which Archinard promptly burned down. The unrepentant Samory would spend the next seven years running rings around the French until they took care of him for good in a surprise attack launched in 1898 — the year of the Fashoda incident. Samory Touré was the grandfather of Sékou Touré, the African nationalist who refused to become a part of "Greater France" when De Gaulle granted independence to France's former colonies in Black Africa in 1962.

### King Glé-Glé's bloody funeral

The French also encountered violent resistance from certain animist tribes. The King of Abomey (formerly Dahomey, now Benin) for instance,

commanded an army feared since the 18th century for its redoubtable corps of women warriors — drawn from the ranks of the king's many wives. Over the years, these "Amazons" had come to include maidens not yet deflowered by the king but his to dispose of as he pleased. According to European "specialists," it was this enforced chastity that accounted for the ladies' ferociousness. Apart from the Amazons, the kingdom of Abomey was also notorious for its human sacrifices.

In the 1880s, the French military sent one of its explorers to negotiate with the ruler of Abomey, King Glé-Glé, who had originally signed a protectorate treaty of sorts with Napoleon III. The explorer in question, Dr. Jean-Marie Bayol, was a navy doctor with a distinguished record in west African exploration and a sheaf of protectorate treaties to his credit. King Glé-Glé being ill, Bayol was obliged to deal with the king's son, "Prince Kondo," who was dismayed to learn that France was now a vulgar republic — so dismayed indeed that he advised Bayol to restore the monarchy if he wished to pursue the negotiations.

When Glé-Glé died, the crown passed to Kondo, who took the name Béhanzin and dubbed himself "Shark of Sharks," terror of his coastal kingdom. The high point of his father's funeral was the ritual human sacrifice of forty boys and forty girls. However, Béhanzin, for all his slavish devotion to barbaric custom, was no fool and certainly no coward. In 1892, when 3,000 French troops were sent into Abomey to eliminate him, they got rather more than they had bargained for. Besides a hail of poison arrows and spears from the Amazons, they also came under fire from Béhanzin, who proved a formidable marksman. For a moment, Colonel Dodds, the Senegalese half-caste officer leading the French attack, was convinced he was up against the Germans, who were France's main rivals in the region at that time. Eventually, Béhanzin was overcome and sent into exile in Algeria together with five of his wives.

## Ashanti gold

The British meanwhile were encountering stiff resistance in the adjacent territory of the Gold

**Above**
Amazons and warriors at the Jardin d'Acclimatation. The defeated "Amazons" and Behanzin's animist warriors often posed for the camera.

Coast (present-day Ghana), separated from Dahomey only by the slim territory of Togo. Things had deteriorated since 1817, when the British traveler and scientific writer Thomas Edward Bowdich (1791-1824) had completed peace negotiations with the Ashanti Empire (now part of Ghana). That agreement had assisted the extension of British influence and the annexation of the Gold Coast. On his return to England in 1818, Bowdich published an account of his expedition, *A Mission from Cape Coast Castle to Ashantee* (1819). In it, he waxed lyrical about his lavish reception from the Ashanti king, whom he described in all his glory, seated beneath silken canopies shimmering with scarlet and other bright colors. He marveled at the finely wrought solid gold necklaces worn by the king's officers and lords and at the canes with golden pommels carried by the royal interpreters. He praised the dignity with which the king held out his hand in a manner that commanded respect and admiration.

Bowdich also remarked on the profusion of drums to be found, some of them decorated with human bones — a detail that should have alerted Bowdich's readers to the dangers of this

*Gone were the days of solitary explorers like Caillié, haunted by the fear of discovery.*
*Gone was any thought of Livingstone, the Bible or Christian charity. The explorer turned conqueror, ready to give as good as he got in the event of a fight.*

gilded kingdom. It seems it did not. People remained fascinated with Ashanti and after Bowdich, various Protestant missionaries also went out there. One of them was Reverend Freeman, who in 1842 founded a mission in Ashanti, only to return with horrific descriptions of human sacrifice. And the Ashanti did not stop at driving Europeans from their own territory. They also carried out raids on the coast of the Gulf of Guinea, occasionally returning with white prisoners, one of whom was a French missionary, Joseph Bonnat, captured in 1869 along with five Swiss colleagues. For the next five years, they were held against their will in Koumassi, capital of Ashanti. Once famous for their gold, the Ashanti people were now notorious for their cruelty. Koumassi, dubbed "the capital of crime" by London newspapers, was taken by British troops in 1874.

Part of the city was burned down and the king was overthrown, but it would take two further campaigns to colonize the whole of the kingdom. In 1900, when Ashanti was finally declared a British trust territory, Koumassi

became the focus of the local cocoa industry. These days, researchers believe that the claims of "human sacrifice" were greatly exaggerated, with many of the ceremonies in question being "merely the execution of villains."

### Glass trinkets and other ammunition

African exploration continued to make new converts in the 1890s, but times had changed. Expeditions were now increasingly armed, and accompanied by an escort of soldiers. Gone were the days of solitary explorers like Caillié, haunted by the fear of discovery. Gone was any thought of Livingstone, the Bible, or Christian charity. The explorer had turned conqueror, ready to give as good as he got in the event of a fight.

One such explorer was the Frenchman Casimir Maistre (1867-1957). In 1892-1893, Maistre was sponsored by the Comité de l'Afrique Coloniale (committee for colonial Africa) to "conclude treaties in the name of France" in unknown regions between Lake Chad and the River Congo. There was no shortage of volunteers: "We were inundated with applications from all sides. Some 4,000 volunteers vied for the honor of joining the mission." Maistre, like his predecessors, took along the usual supply of favors for the natives: "fabrics, glass trinkets, bells, copper wire, mirrors, cowrie shells." But in addition to "some 400 parcels, crates, and waterproof bundles," the supplies also included weapons "to be used as required" by the escort of Senegalese infantrymen. In his book, Maistre freely admits that he did not hesitate to use force.

### The Fourreau-Lamy Mission

**Below**
Ashanti ceremonial sword.

Meanwhile, the Mandjias beat their tom-toms and performed their war dance, a frenzied display of leaps, bounds, and contemptuous gesticulations aimed at frightening us off. We tried to explain that we had come in peace, showed them our pearls and fabrics and promised them other presents. But the tom-toms only struck up more furiously than ever. It was obvious that the natives were all completely drunk and laughing at us, thinking us too frightened to attack. They had no idea that our rifles were offensive weapons. Soon they grew bolder, inching their way forward along the edge of the bush. Just then, a volley of arrows came arcing through the air, almost landing at our feet. The unit moved into defensive positions, rifles loaded and made ready – Kropatchek repeating rifles with eight new cartridges. One last time, I shouted that we didn't want a fight but the Mandjias only replied with another volley of arrows. With no more ado I gave the order to fire. In an instant the air was filled with cries and lamentations and the sounds of a disorderly rout.

Casimir Maistre, *A travers l'Afrique centrale, du Congo au Niger,* 1892-1893

Opposite
The Foureau-Lamy
Mission. No one guessed at
the start of the expedition
that this grand experiment
in cooperation between
"Science and the Military"
would end with one of the
most important battles ever
fought by France in the
conquest of Africa.

Below
Commander Lamy.

Right-hand page
Fernand Foureau.

This French mission of 1898 took the policy of armed expedition to its logical conclusion: conquest by force. Caillié had explored part of the western Sahara on his return from Timbuktu. Clapperton had discovered the eastern part on his return from Tripoli. Only the central part remained unknown. The man chosen to sound its depths was a French civilian explorer with expert knowledge of the desert, Fernand Foureau (1850-1914). He would travel from Algeria to Lake Chad, by way of the treacherous Hoggar and Aïr mountain ranges. In 1881, the French officer Colonel Paul Flatters (1832-1881) had been assassinated by Tuaregs in the Hoggar while conducting a feasibility study aimed at constructing a Trans-Saharan railway. It was decided that Foureau would travel with a military escort under the command of François-Joseph Lamy (1858-1900). In addition to providing protection, Lamy was also ordered to

join up with two other French columns.

On 23 October 1898, the Foureau-Lamy mission pulled out of the Sédatra Oasis in southern Algeria with an impressive cortège of men and pack animals. The horses hauling the canons went first, followed by donkeys loaded with crates of shells. Then came 1,000 camels carrying tents, folding-beds, spare uniforms, the usual supply of favors for the natives, and dates and immense bales of hay in anticipation of the arid desert conditions ahead. The military escort came next: two hundred Senegalese infantrymen and Algerian *spahis* (native Algerian cavalrymen in the French armed forces) commanded by four French officers, including Lamy. Included were six Muslim holy men from the Sahara, in the hope that their presence would discourage hostile receptions from local populations. Two French medical officers also accompanied the mission. Foureau's civilian team included a

*The horses hauling **the canons** went first, followed*
*by donkeys loaded with crates of shells. Then came 1,000 camels carrying tents,*
*folding-beds, spare uniforms...*

student at the Natural History Museum, an astronomer, a photographer, and a French minister with a taste for adventure, Charles Dorian (1828-1923).

### Sand and camel remains

The Tuaregs did nothing as the column pulled out. They merely watched scornfully, and only demanded presents when it halted. That look of disdain, noticed by Foureau, was a bad sign. Plainly the Arabs knew something the French did not — but would soon find out to their cost. As the sun beat down on the burning sand, the piles of camel remains became increasingly frequent. Horses, donkeys, and camels dropped dead between watering holes, and desperate, exhausted Senegalese infantrymen committed suicide. Finally, after a three-month trek, the mission reached Iférouane in the intermediate zone between the Tuareg Sahara and Black Africa. The people there had never seen a white man before, but some of the women at least seemed friendly, even curious. However, at dawn one morning, when the horizon was shrouded in a thick heat haze, men in blue robes attacked the sleeping bivouac. The French retaliated with rifles and guns, firing at random into the horde of Arabs, who eventually retreated. In a last ditch effort to return home alive, the order was given to break camp at once and press on to Agades. The exhausted men collapsed from sunstroke and became delirious. One day, they were ambushed by Tuaregs hidden in the rocks, who set upon them with knives. Lamy opened fire, leaving thirty enemy casualties.

On 14 July 1899, ten months after leaving Algeria, the Mission finally saw its first signs of Black Africa. It entered a village of straw huts, complete with tam-tams and bare-breasted women grinding millet — familiar surroundings for the Senegalese infantrymen, who celebrated with a little dance. Two weeks later, the column reached the town of Agades on the Niger, once the seat of a Tuareg sultanate and almost as mythical as Timbuktu. The last white man to set foot there had been Heinrich Barth almost half a century earlier. Things had changed since then, but not the practice of slavery. Night after night, Negro women kept as slaves by the Tuareg nobility would come to the French camp to watch the Senegalese dance. Much to the annoyance of their "rightful" owners, all of the women were granted their freedom "in accordance with French Republican Law." After that, the local nobility was eager to provide the Foureau-Lamy Mission with enough camels to continue its journey southward. At the head of the column went the former women slaves, now the lovers of the Senegalese infantrymen who had liberated them. Foureau would later describe them as "crazy with joy, always running and dancing ahead of the column."

### The fall of Rabih's Empire

A few miles farther, the cruel, thorny terrain gave way to lush, green vegetation. Then, on 2 November, at the end of a year-long trek, the

*Gentil remarked on the variety of livestock and cereal crops in Chad, and on the local leather and ostrich feather production.*

**Above**
A share issued by the Cameroon rubber and cocoa association in 1926. The start of the 20th century would bring an explosion of French colonial companies with imaginative names. One of them inspired a revolutionary novel by French writer Louis-Ferdinand Céline (1894-1961) titled *Journey to the End of the Night* (*Voyage au bout de la nuit*), which is partly based on his experiences working for a forestry enterprise near Douala.

Foureau-Lamy Mission reached Zinder (the capital of French Niger until 1926-7 when it was replaced by Niamey). It was here that Lamy joined up with the two other French columns, one from Senegal and one from Ubangi-Shari (present-day Central African Republic). Their orders were to eliminate one Rabih-az-Zubayr (French *Rabah*), a Muslim military leader and confirmed Mahdist. Born of a Nilotic people from the Khartoum region, Rabih had been enslaved as a child by az-Zubayr Pasha, a Sudanese prince. Rabih rose to become the prince's second-in-command, supporting his rebellion against the Egyptian administration of

the Sudan in 1878. When Zubayr Pasha was defeated, Rabih fled to central Africa with some 400 followers. By sacking villages on the Shari River and forming alliances with local sultans, he established a military hegemony in the district of Bornu, east of Lake Chad. He also captured Sara men (from the fringes of southern Sudan) whom he sold to slavers in exchange for British-made guns. By the later 1800s, he was no stranger to the French, whose empire-building ambitions in west Africa posed a serious threat to his own. In 1898, the French had had enough of ambushes, kidnappings, and the *Rabah* in general. The officer in charge of eliminating him was Emile Gentil (1866-1914), a French naval officer who became an explorer after working alongside Brazza.

## "Wholesale slaughter"

Having moved northward from the Congo, French forces assembled at Kousseri (in present-day Cameroon) near the Shari River south of Lake Chad. On 21 April, they launched an attack on Rabih's camp about three miles away. The Senegalese infantrymen were particularly merciless, being sworn to take revenge on any slaver who crossed their path. Rabih himself was wounded, then decapitated, by an African who bore his bloody trophy back to the French. In what Gentil would later describe as the "wholesale slaughter" of enemy forces, 1,000 "Rabihst" supporters perished, compared with just fifty French. One of these was Lamy, killed by enemy fire. This marked the French conquest of Chad.

**Opposite**
Gentil, joining up with the Foureau-Lamy Mission. His book *La Chute de l'Empire de Rabah* ("The Fall of Rabih's Empire") paints a horrific picture of the battle of Kousseri: "The coagulated blood of dead bodies, slowly going brown and already giving off that sweet, sickly smell. Birds of prey and vultures descending on the carnage, devouring their gruesome feast. Horrible!"

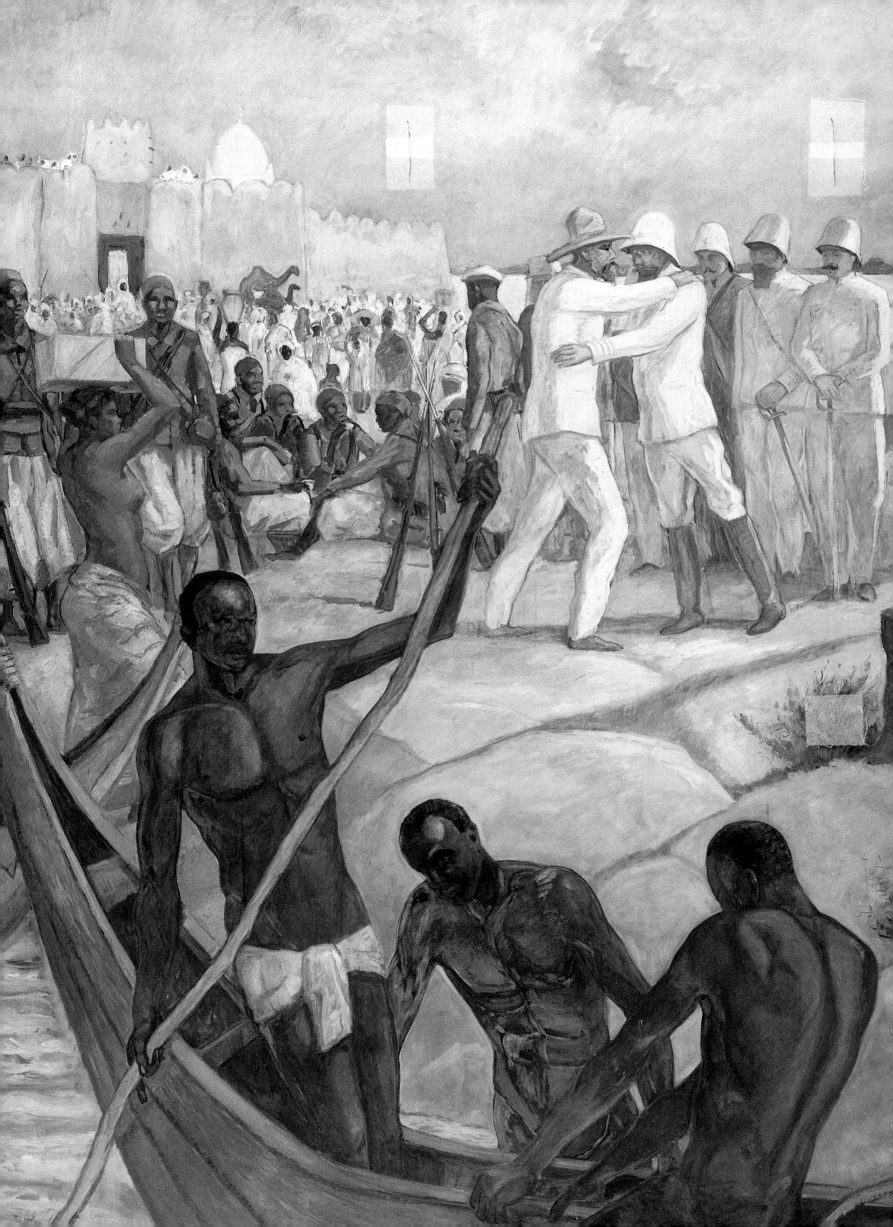

# VI

# Discovering peoples

Until the late 1800s, few people in Europe had ever met a black person, although many had read about African populations in books on exploration. The first real opportunity to see these people in the flesh came around 1880, with a wave of "ethnographic shows" and "African villages" of a kind that would draw the crowds for the next thirty years. They were part of the great Universal Exhibitions that marked the development of Europe in the 1900s, satisfying the taste for novelty that was triggered by the Industrial Revolution. Africans were not the only "curiosities" on offer. There were also Argentine gauchos, Scandinavian Laplanders and Ukrainian Cossacks. One of the major attractions of African "ethnographic shows" was their frequent combination with exhibitions of wild animals, a feature that would later lead to talk of "human zoos." In fact they were nothing of the kind, but as so often happens when things are taken out of context, historical accuracy has become distorted.

# The German Carl Hagenbeck (1844-1913)

was an internationally famous animal dealer and trainer who created the prototype for open-air zoos at Stellingen near Hamburg in 1907. He was also the first to produce and travel with "ethnographical shows" featuring people and animals from the same remote regions. He was soon copied by other

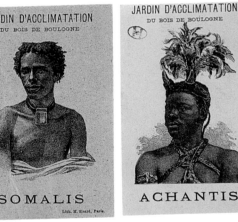

play the part, the Ghanaian Ashantis shown in London not long before had been the real thing. Here were the notorious inhabitants of the city dubbed "the capital of crime" by London newspapers. Its storming by British troops in 1874 had been featured in newspapers throughout the UK, including *The Graphic* and the monthly picture magazine *Illustrated London News*. After London, the Ashantis went on show in Paris.

In 1898, the Belgians built a "Congolese village" right in the center of Antwerp. Three years later, as the band struck up the *Brabançonne* (Belgian national anthem) four more villages were inaugurated at the Brussels International Exhibition. Henry Morton Stanley was one of the dignitaries present. By the time the "villages" were finally taken down, some 430,000 admissions had been sold. The occupants then sailed home again, each with a trunk full of presents and a smattering of foreign words: "watch" and "bowler hat" in the case of the men, "stockings" and "articulated doll" in the case of the ladies.

## Amazons at the Folies-Bergère

In France, a "Congolese Show" organized in Roubaix in 1887 had featured none other than the Makoko, the man who had played such a key role in Brazza's colonizing endeavors. The first "ethnographic shows" had been launched ten years earlier at the Jardin d'Acclimatation in Paris. Founded in 1860 in the Bois de Boulogne (on the borders of Neuilly-sur-Seine, a suburb of northwest Paris) this was not a zoo in the traditional sense but an acclimation center that recreated the natural conditions of wildlife.

The chairman of the board of directors was the

Germans, notably the brothers Möller, who recruited "troupes" of natives in Africa then paid them handsomely to go on tour in Germany and the surrounding countries. From Hamburg to Copenhagen, Willy Möller's "African caravans" drew visitors by the thousands. Far from considering him a charlatan, local experts in anthropology publicly acknowledged the "scientific interest" of Möller's shows. One of his biggest successes was the "Mahdi Warriors" show in 1898, the year in which Kitchener would crush the real "dervishes" in the Sudan. While Möller's Mahdists were actually Kenyans paid to

JARDIN D'ACCLIMATATION

# L'Afrique Mystérieuse

Ouvert de               9 h. à 7 h.

Service direct par le petit train électrique de la Porte-Maillot à l'Afrique Mystérieuse. ∘ ∘

Service direct par le petit train électrique de la Porte-Maillot à l'Afrique Mystérieuse. ∘ ∘

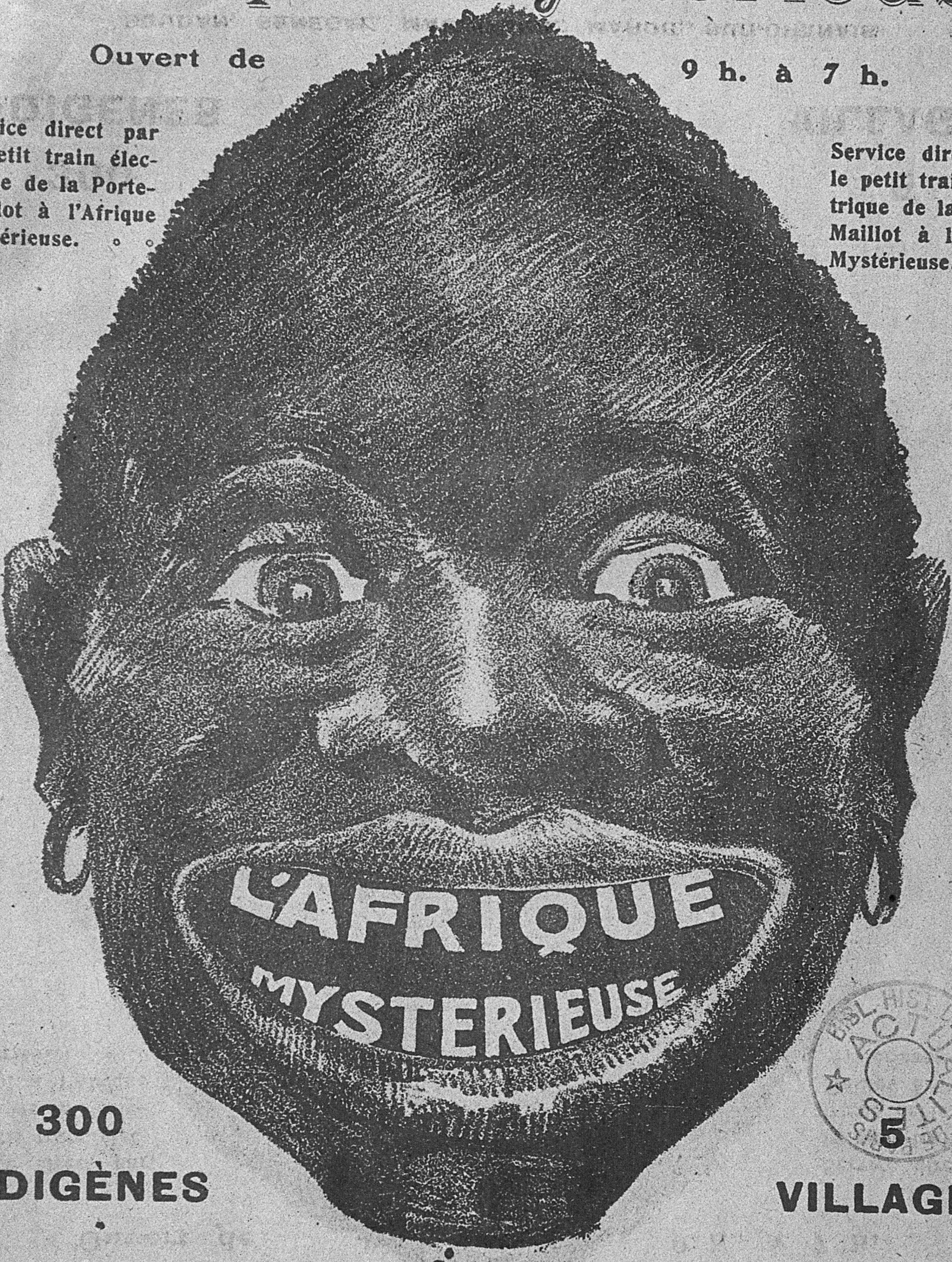

L'AFRIQUE MYSTÉRIEUSE

**300 INDIGÈNES**

**5 VILLAGES**

SOUDAN, SÉNÉGAL, MAURITANIE, MAROC, SUD-ORANAIS

ALGÉRIE, TUNISIE, ÉGYPTE, TRIPOLITAINE, etc.

*Harems, Mosquées, Douars, Camps; Huttes, Tentes, Théâtres*

*There were even "lessons in big cat psychology" held at Vincennes zoo,*
*teaching students* how to behave *when faced by a lion.*

zoologist Isidore Geoffroy Saint-Hilaire (1805-
1861), son of the naturalist Etienne Geoffroy
Saint-Hilaire (1772-1844), who established the
principle of "unity of composition" and founded
teratology, the study of animal malformation.
Isidore now gave his scientific backing to
ethnographic shows linked with animal
exhibitions and staged various exhibitions of
his own at the Jardin d'Acclimatation. The
"specimens" on show attracted large numbers
of the scientific community, including the
distinguished French surgeon Paul Broca
(1824-1880) and Prince Roland Bonaparte
(1858-1924), future president of the Société de
Géographie. Isidore Saint-Hilaire's contribution
to human progress was publicly acknowledged in
the October 1878 issue of *La Nature* magazine.

The writers thanked Saint-Hilaire for "providing
those devoted to the study of the human race
with access to research material they were rarely
adventurous enough to obtain for themselves."
Africans were also recruited by venues with no
scientific pretensions, including Paris theaters
and cabarets. The undisputed stars were the
Dahomeans, especially the "Amazons," whose
valor had been publicly recognized by a number
of French colonial officers. In 1893, the very
serious Société d'Ethnographie went to Dahomey
to recruit more than a hundred Dahomean
men, women, and children for a French tour. In
the same year, the "Amazons" performed in a
show at the Folies-Bergère. But the motives
behind these exhibitions were more than merely
paternalistic. Many people had a genuine
interest in black populations that can in no
way be dismissed as passing curiosity. Indeed,
according to a controversial book recently
published by French authors Jean-Michel
Bergougniou, Remi Clignet, and Philippe
David, it would be an over-simplification "to
reduce these years of contact to a grotesque
stereotype of Whitey-throwing-peanuts-to-
Blackman-over-wire-fence."

**The Tirailleurs Sénégalais**
Whatever might be thought of these "ethnographic
villages," they rarely gave Africans the chance
to discover Europe. But things would change
with the 1914-18 war. In 1910, General Charles
Mangin (1866-1923), a former comrade of
Captain Marchand's (see chapter V), published
an essay in praise of the warlike virtues of the
*Tirailleurs Sénégalais*. And from the beginning of

Afrique Occidentale - SOUDAN
104. Ecole des enfants de troupe
des Tirailleurs indigènes

Collection générale FORTIER, Dakar

hostilities with Germany, tens of thousands of African recruits were sent to the front. In their rare periods of leave, the *Tirailleurs* explored the white man's world, and after the war some were even given the opportunity to visit Germany. Due to a shortage of men, the French general staff sent numbers of Africans to reinforce occupation troops in Bade-Württemberg. According to the historian Gilbert Comte, "for a great many Germans, the very presence of these black troops on German soil was a flagrant and monstrous breach of natural solidarity among Europeans!"

### The real slicing-up of the African cake
The signing of the Treaty of Versailles in 1919 stripped Germany of the African colonies it had worked so hard to acquire. France got Togo and most of the Cameroon. England got the rest of the Cameroon plus Tanganyika (now Tanzania). Belgium got Rwanda and Burundi. The Union of South Africa (now South Africa), whose troops had fought alongside allied forces, got South West Africa (present-day Namibia). What happened next was a massive exercise in character assassination. Germany's reputation as a colonizer was shredded by countries whose own performance in Africa was certainly nothing to

boast about. Indeed, in some respects Germany had done rather better. German missionaries, for instance, especially those from the North German Protestant Mission, were comparable to the French White Fathers.

This was the great "slicing-up of the African cake" that failed to happen at the Berlin Conference in 1885. Setting aside a few minor adjustments, the Treaty of Versailles reshuffled the geopolitical cards in Africa. The colonial borders established in 1919 would remain in place when African countries began winning independence in the 1960s. In the days of the Sultans and Chieftains encountered by early white explorers, Africa was made up of more than 10,000 political entities. In the era of colonization, they had been reduced to just a few dozen.

Much to the delight of philatelists, France divided her Overseas Territories into eight federations, including two in Africa: French West Africa (FWA) and French Equatorial Africa (FEA). The Treaty of Versailles had assigned France and England roughly equal shares in Africa. For the British, however, the undisputed jewel in the empire's crown was India, not Africa. For France, the case was different. Africa accounted for the biggest chunk of its overseas

**Above**
At a time when all well-educated boys collected stamps, more than one young hopeful was inspired by images like these. Indeed, many of those who later made their careers in Africa, from ethnologists to administrators, said that it had all started with their stamp collections.

*The French doctors who were known as "capitaines moustiques" ("mosquito captains") explored Africa's darker side: disease-infested regions rife with sleeping sickness, yellow fever, plague, and leprosy.*

activities, and in the 20th century African culture would become something of a French specialty. But by that time, geographic exploration *per se* had given way to the discovery of peoples and civilizations.

### Lessons in big cat psychology

When Brazza was appointed governor general of the French Congo in 1886, he had been forced to find some of his administrative staff through the small ads. By 1895, the French Third Republic, in recognition of the need for properly qualified colonial administrators, founded the prestigious Ecole Coloniale (Colonial Academy) in Paris. Admission was conditional on passing a stiff entrance examination. The academy closed down in 1959, as numbers of countries began to gain their independence. Today, this neo-Moorish building, flanked by elegant façades, recalls the times when bright-eyed young hopefuls would leave its portals bound for new and exotic horizons. The academy's openness to other cultures was reflected in a comprehensive syllabus that covered ethnology, rural economy, and customary rights. Local dialects were also taught, by two native speakers each destined to become the leader of an African state: Léopold Sédar Senghor (1906-2001), first president of Senegal; and Hamani Diori (1916-1989), first president of independent Niger. There were even "lessons in big cat psychology" held at Vincennes zoo, teaching students how to behave when faced by a lion.

The Ecole Coloniale, renamed the Ecole Nationale de la France d'Outre-Mer in 1934 ("National Academy for French Overseas Studies"), boasted several directors who were distinguished African specialists and educators. One of them was Georges Hardy, Director of Public Education in FWA from 1927-1932, who urged his students to avoid ethnocentricity and to favor "organizations that respected individual freedoms, institutions, and customs."

### The capitaines moustiques

Another prominent French academy was the Ecole de santé de la Marine ("Naval Medical Academy") founded in Bordeaux in 1890 and specializing in tropical medicine. Originally restricted to navy doctors only, it eventually opened its doors to all doctors posted to hospitals overseas, military and civilian alike. These days, former graduates of the academy regard themselves as the forerunners of today's *Medicin sans Frontiers*. To the locals they became "les capitaines moustiques" ("mosquito captains") because of their liberal use of DDT in the fight against malaria.

Many of these doctors worked with the Pasteur Institutes, "exploring" disease-infested regions rife with sleeping sickness, yellow fever, plague, and leprosy – Africa's darker side. One of these doctors was Dr. Eugène Jamot (1879-1937), not a graduate of the Ecole de santé itself but of its training school in Marseilles. At the outbreak of the First World War he left his work at the Pasteur Institute in Brazzaville to fight in the Cameroon. While there he came to realize that, in the area of sleeping sickness the Germans were ahead of the French. The sheer numbers of

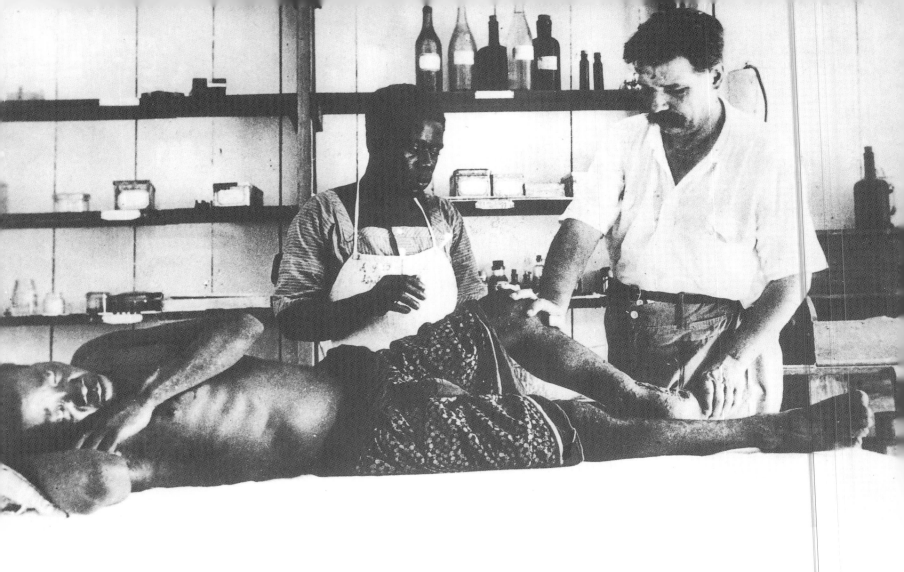

"sleepers" or "dummies" in Africa had meanwhile led Albert Schweitzer in 1913 to found his celebrated clinic in Lambaréné. After the war, Jamot embarked on a mission to "wake up the African peoples" and spent the rest of his life scouring Cameroon, Ubangi-Shari, and Chad in search of victims. He was armed with syringes full of atoxyl, one of the original drugs to combat sleeping sickness, and centrifuges for analyzing blood samples. His efforts were so successful that by 1931, the year of the French Colonial Exhibition, France was ready to announce that sleeping sickness had been completely eradicated in FWA. In Younde, they erected a monument to Jamot. In France, the best they could do was to print a special stamp commemorating his 75th birthday.

Another influential doctor was Jean Bablet (1886-1952), who was so badly bitten by a panther while working as a doctor in FWA that he partially lost the use of his left arm. He nevertheless continued to live an active life, founding histopathological laboratories throughout the French colonies. Today's smart concrete buildings housing the Pasteur Institutes of Younde, Bangui, and Abidjan started out as simple straw huts that the researchers called "paillottes laboratoires". Bablet's discovery of the hepatic lesions specific to yellow fever was a first step in the subsequent development of a vaccine.

## Science and colonial fashions

What is now the *Académie des sciences d'Outre-Mer* ("Academy of Overseas Sciences") first opened in Paris in 1923 as the *Académie des Sciences Coloniales* ("Academy of Colonial Sciences") with a motto that perfectly expressed its purpose: "Knowledge, understanding, and respect." Its founders represented "Parliament, the Military, the Administration, and explorers" and included three future French presidents, several members of the French Academy, various writers but only three former explorers. It was a sign of the times: Africa was moving increasingly into the public domain. Josephine Baker (1906-1975) symbolized the captivating vitality of the Afro-American culture that took Paris by storm in the 1920s. Born in St. Louis, Missouri, she first sashayed onto the

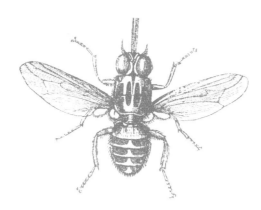

"*Bouet and Roubaud packed their microscopes in their tin trunks and set off by canoe to explore the lagoons of Lower Dahomey. Bouffard hunted alligators and hippopotami to check that they didn't carry Trypanosoma in their blood…* In the end, he was the one who caught sleeping sickness.*"

Colonel (Doctor) Constant Mathis (1871-1956)

stage in Paris at the age of nineteen and became an overnight sensation for her performance in *La Revue Nègre*. Her sensual appeal and exotic beauty earned her the name "Black Venus," captivating Parisian audiences with her electrifying dancing and outrageous costumes. Josephine Baker became one of the Parisian smart set, frequently seen at the newly opened West Indian dance club, the *Bal Colonial* or *Bal Nègre*. This was where writers like Paul Morand (1888-1976) came "to slum it with the Blacks… All our literature was here," he once said of a club that became famous as the first Negro *bal musette* (dance with accordion music) in Paris. Morand's account of his travels through Africa, *Paris-Tombouctou* (1929) was an instant bestseller. In it, he paid tribute to the "infinitely superior" vitality of black culture that remained "true to its instincts." "What we ask of Africa today is to show us what the world was like in its age of innocence," he said.

The call of Africa was irresistible, even for an esthete like André Gide (1869-1951), who could by no stretch of the imagination be called a "travel writer." At the age of fifty-six he left his pampered

**Above**

The stamp says, "Dr Jamot, the man who wiped out sleeping sickness." All the same, the medical establishment did not endorse Jamot's candidacy for the Nobel Prize for medicine in 1931. That was the year of the Colonial Exhibition, when France announced that sleeping sickness had been completely eradicated in FWA. Jamot pioneered "sleeper houses" very like leper clinics for seriously ill patients, and used to call patients for blood tests on a tom-tom. But he had none of Schweitzer's diplomacy and frequently fell out with the Administration.

**Above**

A tsetse fly, the bloodsucking African insect that transmits sleeping sickness (encephalitis lethargica).

*Born in St. Louis, Missouri, Josephine Baker first sashayed onto the stage in Paris at the age of 19 and became an overnight sensation for her electrifying performance in La Revue Nègre.*

Parisian existence for the depths of equatorial Africa, where he hunted for the first time in his life and consorted with the natives. Indeed, when asked by the colonial Administration whether he preferred to be carried by porters or walk with the escort of sixty or so Africans, Gide chose the latter. What he concluded from his trip was that "the less a white man is intelligent, the more a black man seems stupid to him." In the book he published on his return to France, *Voyage au Congo* (1927; *Travels in the Congo*), he criticizes French colonial policies and displays a compassion for mankind that marked the closing years of his life.

Journalist Albert Londres' *Terre d'Ebène* (1929) was another stinging condemnation of crimes committed in the name of colonialism. In 1928, Londres (1884-1932) spent four months in Africa traveling from Senegal to the Congo. What he saw there convinced him of the urgent need for radical reform. He was especially outspoken about the exploitation of black workers on the new railway linking Brazzaville and Pointe-Noire. Londres' comments were not confined solely to the French but extended to certain local potentates: "What happened to all those slaves when the slave trade was (officially) abolished by European states? Were they abolished too? No, they simply stayed where they were, with their buyers. Only now they are no longer known as 'slaves' but 'house servants.' Now it is Blacks enslaved by Blacks." On the whole, however, Londres had fond memories of the Africans who made a white man feel "rather like the good Lord out on a stroll." He and Paul Morand traveled together for a while before Morand left for Timbuktu.

## The Black Cruise

Naturally, the advertising industry was quick to take advantage of the African wave sweeping through France, by devious means if necessary. Take, for instance, the automobile "cruises" organized by André Citroen (1878-1935), the first to invent a front-wheel-drive car. What he needed was a place, with virtually no paved roads, where he could put his cars through their paces. Africa fit the bill perfectly. In 1922 Georges Marie Haardt, general manager of the Citroen factories, set out from Touggourt (Algeria) with a team of ten people and made it to Timbuktu (Sudan) in just twenty days. Two years later came

**Preceding page and below**
Paul Colin (1889-1963) was Josephine Baker's favorite designer, and the graphic brains behind this neo-cubist poster. After *La Revue nègre*, Baker starred in *Princess Tom-Tom* (1935), a film about a beautiful African woman who is taken to Paris by a writer but eventually decides to return home.

the first "Black Cruise," a sporting promotion with government backing aimed at establishing a safe, quick link between mainland France and equatorial Africa. In June 1925, eight half-tracks arrived in Madagascar, having departed from Colomb-Bechar (northwest Algeria) the previous November, a distance of more than 17,500 miles across Africa. Two "laboratory cars" and two "camera cars" returned with 25,000 yards of film and 6,000 photographs. Citroen's "official painter," Alexander Iacovleff (1887-1938) also went along, returning with images in the "colonial art" style that was so popular at the time. It was a form of art that sought to emphasize the "exotic naturalism" of people and scenery, and Iacovleff was a past master of the style

## Connoisseurs of "Black art"

In the 1910s, a Hungarian art dealer, Joseph Brummer, was surprised to find a strange African mask at the back of an auto parts shop. The young assistant explained that he occasionally came by such "Negro curiosities" through rubber suppliers to the tire industry. Brummer bought the mask and asked to be notified of any future deliveries. The assistant was Paul Guillaume (1891-1934), who rose to become a leading figure among the cultural players and Parisian art dealer-collectors of the early 20th century. With his usual flair for business, he immediately placed advertisements offering to buy any "Negro *objets*" acquired by travelers to Africa. From these humble beginnings came the first Parisian gallery of African art, opened by Paul Guillaume in the Rue de Miromesnil in downtown Paris.

At about the same time, the French Fauvist painter, Maurice de Vlaminck (1876-1958) bought a round of drinks for all the customers in a suburban bar in Paris. By way of thanks, two strangers who were probably sailors gave him several Dahomean statuettes. Vlaminck's enthusiasm for *"African objets"* (which weren't yet known as art) was shared by his painter friends, notably fellow Fauvists André Derain (1880-1954) and Henri Matisse (1869-1954). On one occasion, a friend of the family gave Vlaminck a Fang mask that he then sold to his studio companion Derain to raise cash at the end of the

*Most people called it "African art," but some also knew it as "primitive art" or "tribal art."*

month. Pablo Picasso (1881-1973) and Matisse went into raptures over the mask when they saw it in Derain's studio. So started the craze for African art, which, from that point onward, was the inspiration for every Fauvist and Cubist painter in Europe. Picasso, for instance, would later have his "African period." It was irrelevant that not one of these artists had ever set foot in Africa and most of them did not know a single black person. For once, artists agreed with the "bourgeoisie" about what most people called "African art," but some also knew as "primitive art" or "tribal art." When Paul Guillaume announced that African sculpture was "the rejuvenating sperm of the 20th century," his affluent clientele nodded approvingly. Painters meanwhile declared "the autonomy of the plastic artifact," which had a "self-sufficient fullness" beyond sociological or ethnological considerations. This brought howls of protest from sociologists, who openly condemned such "flagrant appropriation" of African art with wanton disregard for its original socio-cultural context.

### Primitive clutter

There were already a number of ethnographic museums in Europe. France, for example, on the occasion of the Universal Exhibition of 1878, had founded the "Musée d'Ethnographie" (now part of the Musée de l'Homme) on Chaillot hill in Paris. Its purpose was to provide researchers with a collection of "objects originally from cultures unknown to Europeans." Due to lack of resources, this turned out to be a real assortment of clutter. Picasso, who visited the

museum in his African period, would describe it to his friend André Malraux (1901-1976) as "disgusting... A real flea market. And the smell!" This is not to say that he was not seduced by what he saw: "I could not tear myself away. I realized that all this was very important: something was happening to me. These masks were no ordinary sculptures... Spirits, the unconscious, emotion – it was all the same." The quote is taken from Malraux's *Picasso's Mask*.

French "esthetes" and "ethnologists" today remain as divided as ever over the issue of African art. After his election in 1995, President Chirac gave the go-ahead for a monumental project close to his heart: a new museum totally dedicated to tribal art (what the French euphemistically call "les arts premiers"). Many ethnographic curators in the Musée de l'Homme and the Musée des Arts d'Afrique et d'Océanie shuddered at the thought of handing over their cherished collections (plus some of the more "primitive" pieces in the Louvre) to the new museum, which is due to open on the Quai Branly in Paris in 2004. For them, it is a profanity to exhibit ethnographic artifacts under the same roof as the works of great masters. They argue that such a policy will only increase speculative trading in the so-called "primitive" art market, encouraging Africans to part with their last remaining treasures.

### Booty and collections

Despite their best intentions, white ethnologists have indeed plundered the African continent, accumulating vast collections of African *objets*. Explorers, especially the military, first started

bringing back "souvenirs" in the 19th century. But things went much faster after 1931, year of the Dakar-Djibouti Mission launched by Josephine Baker at the Trocadero in Paris. The team leader was Marcel Griaule (1898-1956), a French ethnologist who had made his reputation studying the Dogons of Mali. The aim of this multidisciplinary expedition was to drive across Africa from west to east by way of Senegal, French Sudan (Mali), Niger, Upper Volta, Dahomey, Nigeria, Cameroon, Ubangi-Shari, the Anglo Egyptian Sudan, and Ethiopia. In a bid to guarantee the cooperation of colonial administrators, the Mission had the official backing of the French government. The expedition brochure was written by French novelist Michel Leiris (1901-1990), then the Mission "secretary and archivist." It was aimed at the colonial authorities and stated that "The objects that say the most about a civilization are ordinary,

everyday things. A collection of ethnographic objects is not a collection of works of art."
Two years later the Mission returned with a rich haul of "booty" – to use the word coined in all innocence by Paul Rivet (1876-1958), founder of the Musée de l'Homme. The haul included 3,500 *"objets"* ranging from a bone hair pin to "fortune-telling sticks" (bamboo sticks thrown, then "read" by seers), plus 6,000 photographs, 3,300 yards of film and 200 recordings. Leiris had very mixed feelings about the whole business. In his account of the trip, *L'Afrique fantôme* (1934), he wrote that every night he used to "take samples" from a fetish, "a sort of brownish pig that looked like nougat but was actually made of congealed blood and weighed more than thirty lbs." Griaule meanwhile conducted his ethnographic research like a police investigation, complete with "confrontations" and "incriminating evidence."

**Above**
American surrealist photographer Man Ray (1890-1976) juxtaposed white models with African masks to create an ironic, sensual illustration of the west's appropriation of black art. Pictured here is Alice Prin (a.k.a. Kiki de Montparnasse, Man Ray's mistress of fourteen years).

**Following double page**
The imposing landscape of the Bandiagara country peopled by the Dogons on the borders of Mali and Burkina-Faso, along the Bandiagara cliff. What 1930s French ethnologist Marcel Griaule found especially fascinating about the Dogons was their culture and ancient belief system, which was largely untouched by Islam.

*But things went much faster after 1931, year of the*
*Dakar–Djibouti Mission launched by*
# Josephine Baker *at the Trocadero in Paris.*

### Contact with local communities

The social sciences came into being at roughly the same time as colonization. Indeed, social scientists owe a great deal to colonization, even though what they mainly highlighted later were its negative aspects. In the 1950s, French ethnologists were replaced by sociologists like Georges Balandier (b. 1920), who went out to Africa to study the social disruption caused by the white man's sudden presence in traditional societies. Ethnologists had observed indigenous populations in their natural state. Sociologists would assess how those populations had been transformed as a result of contact with the outside world. This was a lengthy process, often requiring years of commitment on the part of researchers as well as a certain amount of introspection due to the degree of cultural fusion involved.

Scientific missions did not cease when African states began winning their independence. Indeed, things came full circle in 1983, when Nigel Barley, a British anthropologist and assistant keeper at the British Museum in London, published his first book, *The Innocent Anthropologist*, a witty and informative account of fieldwork by European anthropologists in Cameroon.

### Parisians in pith helmets

In May 1931, French President Gaston Doumergue walked down the Grande-Avenue-des-Colonies-Françaises near the Bois de Vincennes on his way to inaugurate the International Colonial Exhibition. With the exception of Germany, most of the European countries to produce noteworthy explorers had been invited, including Italy (now under Mussolini), Belgium, and Portugal. Great Britain, on the verge of creating the Commonwealth, only put in a limited appearance. The Italian stand praised Italy's achievements in Eritrea and Somalia; the Belgian stand focussed on the Congo, the largest of all the European African colonies; and the grandiose Portuguese stand recalled the country's former glory in a continent where its only remaining colonies were Angola and Mozambique. The admission ticket featured a

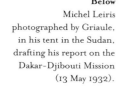

**Below**
Michel Leiris
photographed by Griaule,
in his tent in the Sudan,
drafting his report on the
Dakar-Djibouti Mission
(13 May 1932).

**Above**
Marcel Griaule (1898–
1956) seen here developing
his photographs on the
Dakar-Djibouti Mission.
He was one of a group of
Africanists whose research
helped to distinguish
ethnology as a discipline
apart from sociology. A
student of Marcel Mauss,
Griaule was more inclined
toward empirical research,
establishing the consistency
of African cultures through
an analysis of myth, ritual,
and cosmogony.

white man in a pith helmet, and for visitors who wanted to get into the mood, pith helmets were on sale on every street corner outside. In just four months, the exhibition was visited by a total of eight million people: four million Parisians, three million provincial French, and one million foreigners.

Crowds gathered to see the lions and elephants in the zoological park that was created for the occasion. There were canoe races on the Daumesnil Lake. Outside the FWA stand, one of the biggest "African villages" ever built was home to dozens of Africans who sang, danced, wove, cooked, and even "hunted." The exhibition guide described them as "the finest in the world." One of the exhibition participants was the powerful "Ligue Maritime et Coloniale" ("Maritime and Colonial League"), a 550,000-strong membership association covering, most notably, the teaching profession. Since 1925,

"the building of the French colonial empire" had been part of the history syllabus. School textbooks sung the praises of explorers, Brazza in particular. At the end of their visit, the ostentatious new "Cité des Informations" was a compulsory visit for school children of every age. This state-of-the art information center featured all the latest news about the Empire transmitted by the Havas Agency, and flashing wall charts that showed the production areas of leading African exports.

### Papaya, manioc and coffee

One of the entries in Diderot's *Encyclopédie* was an article on Melegueta pepper (or Grains of Paradise) which had been used as a condiment from early times. However common, remarked the writer, nobody had ever bothered to describe Melegueta pepper, proving that "what motivates people is greed, not thirst for scientific

**Above and right**
The traditional pith helmet was made of pith bark (cork) covered in canvas twill. It became all the rage in Paris during the Colonial Exhibition of 1931 (*above*). Today's bush hat in thick cotton has none of the chic of the pith helmet, but none of the "imperialist" associations either.

**Right-hand page**
European ladies at Mombasa Station, c. 1909.

knowledge." In fact, botanical specimens brought back by travelers would not be properly described for many years. The existence of several vernacular names added to the confusion, and some authors chose to use familiar European terms such as "apples," "plums," "beans," "peas," or "seeds." The papaya, for instance, originally native to the Americas, was described by a late 17th-century traveler to the Gold Coast as "a round fruit rather like a small melon and tasting very like cauliflower." The description and preparation of a given plant in its African environment could vary considerably from one author's work to another. The 20th century introduced a more rigorous approach, as scientists carried out studies to determine the properties of peanuts, yams, manioc, millet, sweet potatoes, and

sorghum. One of their findings was that a good many African staple foods were originally native to America. Peanuts, for instance, were first brought to Africa on the slave ships. Manioc (or ground Cassava), originally from Brazil and Paraguay, is thought to have reached Africa in the 16th century. It was readily adopted by coastal populations who made it the basis of their cooking, but inland communities only grew cassava under pressure from the colonial authorities, who saw it as a panacea for famine. Likewise, coffee, (originally native to west Africa) especially *C. robusta,* was first grown commercially in east Africa by the British in 1880 in response to a worldwide demand that the Indies could no longer satisfy. The first plantations are thought to have been the work of Protestant missionaries in Kenya, soon followed

by the Germans in Tanganyika.

In 1929, French explorer and botanist August Chevalier (1873-1956) founded a Chair and laboratory of colonial agronomy at the Muséum National d'Histoire Naturelle in Paris. Over the course of repeated trips to Senegal, the Sudan, Chad and Ubangi-Shari, Chevalier built up a huge collection of tropical woods and seeds. He is remembered for his seminal work on botany, *Revue d'agriculture coloniale et de géographie botanique*. The museum would later play a leading role in the research and conservation of equatorial environments through its involvement with the La Maboke Research Station (Central African Republic). The station was founded in 1962 by distinguished French botanist and mycologist, Professor Roger Heim (1900-1979), who was Director of the museum from 1951 to 1965.

## Benefits of medicinal plants

Tropical medicine, despite everything it has done for Africa, has too often ignored the healing properties of the indigenous pharmacopoeia. Before the days of hospitals and health centers, African communities relied exclusively on traditional healers and medicinal plants. Time and again, missionaries and medical aid workers found that many of these plants, when correctly administered, were equal in efficacy to chemical drugs. It is no accident that a French medical NGO currently active in Senegal chose to call itself "Le Kinkeliba" after the vernacular name of a sub-Saharan plant used to make infusions to treat hypertension and malaria.

These days traditional African remedies are the focus of research in centers throughout the

**Following double page**
Coffee harvesting in Madagascar, an island with a turbulent history off the east coast of Africa. It was discovered in 1500 by Portuguese navigator Diego Dias and originally consisted of a patchwork of rival kingdoms. In 1643, France founded Fort Dauphin in the south of the island, but by the 19th century various dynasties were seeking alliances with the French or the British. In 1885, following the signing of a protectorate treaty with France, the island became a French colony within the Franco-African economic community. Today Madagascar is famous for vanilla, cloves, coffee, and green pepper.

PLANTES MÉDICINALES. (Aloë socrotina)

Aloès.

Récolte de la sève.

Floraison.

VÉRITABLE EXTRAIT DE VIANDE LIEBIG.

*Coffee was first planted in east Africa by the British in 1880, in response to a worldwide demand that the Indies could no longer satisfy.*

continent. The works of Professor Abayomi Sofowora of the University of Ife (Nigeria) are supported by the Ecole de Pharmacie de Lausanne and the Académie Suisse des Sciences Naturelles (Switzerland), the University of Illinois, and the Tokyo College of Pharmacy. Professor Sofowora is a member of the Regional Expert Committee on Traditional Medicine in the WHO African region, formed in June 2001.

## The camera's eye

"In my view you cannot claim to have seen something until you have photographed it," wrote Emile Zola (1840-1902) in 1900, a time when photographs or photo-based engravings were already a feature of every exploration periodical. At the turn of the century, no self-respecting traveler would have dreamed of leaving without his Zeiss or reflex camera. Henri Gouraud (1867-1946), the French officer who finally captured Samory Touré in 1898, was almost as keen on photography as he was on geography. In addition to writing several published accounts of his missions, he also took some 20,000 snaps documenting his expeditions (now stored at the French Ministry of Foreign Affairs). Gouraud's comprehensive photographic record makes use of every technique at his disposal (salted paper prints, stereoscopic views, autochromes) and all

available manpower — he often enlisted the help of his men.

In the early 1900s people came from all over the world, not just the colonizing nations, to look at Africa through the lenses of their cameras. These were the "image hunters," a new breed of traveler who would include such famous people as Dian Fosse and Leni Riefenstahl. The first professional photographer to venture to the heart of the Congo was the Pole Kasimir Ostoja Zagourski (1880-1941). His outstanding photographic reportage from the 1920s and 1930s captures the life styles of some of Africa's remotest communities. Shot after shot portrays the ceremonies and objects of the lost tribes who accepted him, creating a record of context and ritual made up of initiations, circumcisions, masked dances, music, and hunting.

Another strong-minded personality was Vivienne de Watteville (1900-1957). The daughter of an English woman and a Swiss naturalist, she accompanied her father on a trip to east Africa in 1923, where he was mauled to death by a big cat. This would have been quite enough to put most people off Africa and its wildlife for good. But not de Watteville, who became passionate about big cats and deplored their plight in captivity: "Behind that terribly dumb and patient look in the eyes of performing animals were unimagined depths of hopeless misery."

**Left-hand page**
The bitter juice of south and east African aloes was said to have purgative properties (advertising image).

**Above**
In the 1930s, French households cooked with peanut oil from Senegal. In the days of the Occupation, they had to make do with rape oil.

**Following double page**
Poster advertising the benefits of winter cruises.

Yet the closer you come to wild animals, the greater the
feeling of frustration. The stalk is successful, the prize so near;
but whether as a hunter you kill it or as a photographer you take
your picture of it, it has eluded you to the end. The trophy
is dead, the picture is nothing. I believe that everyone who has held
the spoor through long hours of alternate hope and despair,
be he never so keen a collector, feels before all else as I felt
when I lay watching the wildebeest, that the real reward would
be to go among them without their minding.

Vivienne de Watteville, *Speak to the Earth*, 1935

She departed for Kenya with assorted cameras, a gramophone, and a stock of tea. Animal lover though she was, she could nevertheless understand the passion for hunting: "We hunt what we love because we want to possess it. It may not be humane but at least it is human." Personally, she preferred lying in wait with a camera rather than a gun. Her aim was "nature photography": "The whole essence of the game was to watch animals as closely as possible without disturbing them, and to retreat before they had any idea that one was there." Better than anyone else, Vivienne de Watteville described the technical difficulties of an art that required her to see without being seen, always approaching from downwind: "Here was I... almost able to touch those wildebeest; yet one movement of mine would have made them... stampede in terror."

## Gorillas in the Mist

The American Dian Fossey (1932-1985) not only photographed mountain gorillas, she also "talked" to them by copying their "gorilla vocalizations." After devoting years of her life to the study of these gentle giants, she became the world's leading authority on the mountain gorilla. The person who actually discovered them was Robert von Beringe (1865-1940), a captain in the Colonial German Army in East Africa. On 17 October 1902, he was on a mission to define the borders between the German colony of Rwanda and the Belgian Congo, when he shot two large apes of unknown breed in the Virunga volcanoes. German researchers classified these intriguing silver backs as a new form of gorilla, which they named *Gorilla gorilla beringei,* after the man who discovered them. Rwanda then became

**Above**
African enthusiasts came from all walks of life. This picture was taken by Prince Henri d'Orléans (1867-1901), explorer and grandson of King Louis-Philippe of France (1773-1850).

**Following double page**
While whites were busy putting the natives to work on roads and railways, the camera focussed on the slow, peaceful pace of Africa's "other side."

*African exploration in the 19th century was a largely male domain — women were conspicuous by their absence. The next century would bring some* formidable women adventurers *into the picture, driven more by sociological concerns than geographic curiosity.*

a Belgian protectorate, and for the next few years the mountain gorillas in the Virunga volcanoes became the prey of numerous hunters. Finally, in 1925, Carl Akeley (1864-1926), a biologist and conservationist at the American Museum of Natural History, persuaded King Albert I of Belgium to create Africa's first national park to protect mountain gorillas. Akeley had hoped to study his protégés, but he died of malaria after just four months in the cold damp climate of the Virungas.

British anthropologist and archaeologist Dr.

imagine a more unlikely candidate for fieldwork at an altitude of 10,000 feet, searching for gorillas in the mists and ravines of the Virunga Mountains. Nevertheless, following that meeting with Leakey, she set out to explore the subject that later became her vocation. In 1966, she began a hermit-like existence in Zaire, tentatively approaching her first male gorillas, some of which weighed more than 160 lbs. *Gorillas in the Mist* (1983) is Fossey's highly personal, detailed account of how she bonded with the apes. It recalls the day when, after sitting

Louis Leakey (1903-1972) was one of the many scientists who shared Akeley's interest in *Gorilla gorilla beringei*. In 1963, Leakey happened to meet Dian Fossey when she was on holiday in east Africa. Fossey at the time was an occupational therapist with weak lungs and no formal training in animal behavior. It would be difficult to

among the gorillas for a while, a young male she named Peanuts came over and touched her. "I've been accepted by a gorilla," she wrote. It describes the "gorilla vocabulary" she used to communicate: "I am here, I am harmless." The film adaptation of the book was released posthumously in 1987.

After civil war broke out in Zaire, Fossey continued her pioneering work from the Karisoke Research Center in Rwanda. This later became the headquarters of her anti-poaching patrols, organized to prevent the continuing slaughter of a highly endangered species. The hands and feet of gorillas were especially sought after, the heads as wall decorations and the feet as ashtrays. As part of her war against poaching, Fossey was a frequent contributor to *National Geographic* and lectured extensively in the U.S. But her militant activities made enemies, and on 27 December 1985 she was found hacked to death in her cabin at Karisoke. The fight continues today from the Dian Fossey Gorilla Fund International, which she founded in 1978. Currently there are estimated to be some 650 gorillas in the Virunga Massif and Bwindi (Rwanda and Uganda).

## Leni Riefenstahl among the Nubas

African exploration in the 19th century was a largely male domain, featuring heroes like Caillié, Livingstone, and Brazza. Women were conspicuous by their absence. The next century would bring some formidable women adventurers into the picture, driven more by sociological concerns than geographic curiosity. Vivienne de Watteville and Dian Fossey were among those who left their mark on Africa in the 20th century. Actress and producer Leni Riefenstahl (1902-2003) was another. However controversial, she is best remembered as one of the only truly great female directors in film history. She won prizes across Europe for *Triumph of the Will*, her documentary about the 1934 Nazi congress at Nuremberg. *Olympia*, her film of the Berlin Olympics, was declared a triumph on its release in 1938. By the time she went out

*The equatorial forests through which Brazza and Serpa Pinto hacked their way with billhooks are now slashed through by* macadamized roads.

to Africa in 1960, she was already famous, to many notorious.

After the war, Riefenstahl read of the Nubas, a remote and largely inaccessible tribe in the southern Sudan. They were tall, with perfect bodies, and had lived tucked away in the mountains since their ancestors had fled there to escape slave traffickers. At the age of sixty, Leni Riefenstahl embarked on a new career. Having obtained permission from Khartoum and learned the rudiments of the vernacular language, she set off alone to win the acceptance of isolated tribes living outside the sphere of "civilization." She succeeded. Between 1963 and 1975, the images she captured of intimate Nuba initiation rituals bear witness to her talents as an ethnographic researcher. First published by *Life magazine*, they won worldwide acclaim.

### From empty spaces to red zones

In 1983, civil war in the Sudan broke out. A few years earlier, Rwanda, where Dian Fossey sought refuge, suffered one of the worst genocides in the history of Africa. At Cabora Bassa, in Mozambique, and in Inga, Zaire, two immense dams span the rivers that Livingstone and Stanley sailed up at such cost. The equatorial forests through which Brazza and Serpa Pinto hacked their way with billhooks are now slashed through by macadamized roads. The feuding kingdoms and temperamental monarchs that gave such a mixed reception to Park and Barth have been replaced by the ever-present threat of ethnic wars and hostilities between traditional monarchies.

From the Sudan to the Congo, Somalia to Angola, the "unknown lands" that were marked by blank spaces on ancient charts have become the "red zones" of modern maps. Africa has been discovered, air travel has brought it closer, and Africa has in effect become smaller. Gone are those wide open spaces where intrepid explorers discovered a freedom shared only by the animals that reveled in the new dawn light.

**Below and right**
Leni Riefstenhal, who, after flirting with the Nazis and glorifying Aryan purity, whiteness, and blondness, found unexpected happiness creating a photographic tribute to African peoples.

**Following double page**
Masked Dama tribesmen photographed by Marcel Griaule.

# Bibliography

## Accounts by explorers and travelers

### Original editions

Baines, Thomas, *Explorations in South-West Africa: Being an Account of a Journey in the Years 1861 and 1862 from Walvisch Bay, on the Western Coast, to Lake Ngami and the Victoria Falls* (London: Longman, Green, Roberts & Green, 1864).

Baker, Samuel, *The Albert N'Yanza, Great Basin of the Nile, and Explorations of the Nile Sources* (London: Macmillan and Co, 1866).

Barth, Henry *Travels and Discoveries in North and Central Africa: being a journal of an expedition undertaken under the auspices of H.B.M's Government, in the years 1849-1855*, 4 vols. (London: Appleton, New York & Longmans, 1857).

Binger, Louis, *Du Niger au golfe de Guinée, à travers le pays de Kong et le Mossi*, 2 vols. (Paris: Hachette, 1892).

Burton, Sir Richard, *The Lake Regions of Central Africa* (London: Longman, 1860).

Caillié, René, *Journal d' un voyage à Temboctou et à Jenné dans l'Afrique centrale, précédé d'observations faites chez les Maures Braknas, les Nalous et autres peuples, pendant les années 1824, 1825, 1826, 1827, 1828*, 3 vols. and atlas (Paris: Imprimerie Royale: 1830).

Dubois, Félix, *La Vie au continent noir. Scènes de la vie d'exploration. Récit d' un voyage en Guinée française et dans le pays du Haut-Niger, accompli par Félix Dubois et le peintre Adrien Marie sous la direction du capitaine Brosselard-Faidherbe* (Paris: J. Hetzel, 1893).

_ , *Tombouctou la Mystérieuse* (Timbuktu the Mysterious) (Paris: Flammarion, 1897; London: Heinemann, 1897).

Gallieni, Joseph, *Voyage au Soudan français* (Paris: Hachette, 1885).

Lander, Richard and John, *Journal of an expedition to explore the course and termination of the Niger, with a narrative of a voyage down that river to its termination*, 3 vols. (London: John Murray, 1832).

Lenz, Oskar, *Reise durch Marokko, die Sahara und den Sudan Timbouctou* (Travels in Morocco, the Sahara and the Sudan) 2 vols. (Brockhaus, 1892).

Livingstone, David, *Missionary Travels and Researches in South Africa* (London: Murray, 1857).

Livingstone, David and Charles, *Narrative of an Expedition to the Zambezi and its Tributaries 1865* (London: Murray, 1865).

Livingstone, David, *The Last Journals of David Livingstone in Central Africa from 1865 to His Death* (London: Murray, 1874).

Maistre, Casimir, *A travers l'Afrique centrale, du Congo au Niger* (Paris: Hachette, 1895).

Mollien, Gaspard, Théodore, *Voyage dans l'intérieur de l'Afrique, aux sources du Sénégal, fait en 1818, par ordre du gouvernement français* (Travels in the interior of Africa to the sources of the Senegal and the Gambia performed by command of the French government), 2 vols. (Imprimerie Veuve Courlier, 1820; London 1820).

Park, Mungo, *Travels in the Interior Districts of Africa performed under the Direction and Patronage of the African Association in the years 1795, 1796 and 1797*, 2 vols. (London: G. & W. Nicol, 1799).

Speke, John Hanning, *Journal of the discovery of the source off the Nile by Captain J. H. Speke*, second edition (Edinburgh and London: William Blackwood and Sons, 1864).

Schweinfurth, Georg, *Im Herzen von Afrika. Reisen und Entdeckungen im Centralen Aequatorial-Afrika während der Jahre 1868 bis 1871* (The Heart of Africa: Three years' travels and adventures in the unexplored regions of Central Africa from 1868 to 1871), 2 vols. (Leipzig & London: F.A. Brockhaus & Sampson Low, Marston, Low, and Searle, 1874).

Serpa Pinto, Alexandre, *Como eu atravessei Africa do Atlantico ao Mar Indico, viagem de Benguella à contra-costa* (How I crossed Africa: from the Atlantic to the Indian Ocean, through unknown countries; discovery of the Great Zambezi affluents etc.) (London: Sampson Low, Marston, Searle, and Rivington, 1881).

Stanley (Morton), Henry, *How I found Livingstone* (London: Sampson & Low, 1872).

_, *Through the Dark Continent* (London: G. Newnes, 1899).

_, *In Darkest Africa, or, The Quest, Rescue and Retreat of Emin, Governor of Equatoria* (New York: C. Scribner's Sons; Toronto: Presbyterian News, 1890).

### Recent Editions

Battuta, Ibn, *Travels in Asia and Africa, 1325-1354* (London: Routledge & Kegan Paul, 1983).

Brazza, Pierre Savorgnan de, *Au cœur de l'Afrique, vers la source des grands fleuves*, "Petite Bibliothèque Payot /Voyageurs" Collection (selected accounts published in Le Tour du monde from 1887-1888, titled Voyages dans l'Ouest africain.) (Paris: Phébus, 1992).

Burton, Richard, and Speke, John, *Aux sources du Nil. La Découverte des Grands Lacs africains 1857-1863* (anthology of illustrated accounts by Burton and Speke published in Le Tour du monde) (Paris: Phébus, 1988).

Caillié, René, *Voyage à Tombouctou*, 2 vols. (Paris: La Découverte, 1989).

Douville, Jean-Baptiste, *Un Voyage au Congo, 1827-1828* (Paris: La Table Ronde, 1991).

Africanus, Leo, *History and Description of Africa* (London: Hakluyt Society, 1896; Reprint New York: Franklin [1963]).

Livingstone, David, *Missionary Travels and Researches in South Africa* (Santa Barbara: Narrative Press, 2001).

Mollien, Gaspard-Théodore, *L'Afrique occidentale en 1818 vue par un explorateur français* (Paris: Calmann-

Lévy, 1967).
Park, Mungo, *Travels in the Interior Districts of Africa* (Ware, UK: Wordsworth, 2002).

### 20th century publications

Balandier, Georges, *Afrique ambiguë* (Ambiguous Africa: cultures in collision) (Paris: Plon, 1957, also "Pocket" Collection; London: Chatto & Windus, 1966).

Barley, Nigel, *The Innocent Anthropologist* (London: British Museum Publications, c. 1983).

Fossey, Dian, *Gorillas in the Mist* (London: Phoenix, 2001).

Gide, André, *Voyage au Congo* (Travels in the Congo) (Paris: Editions de la NRF, 1927, also "Folio" Collection; London: Penguin Travel Library series, Penguin 1986).

Haardt, Georges-Marie, and Audouin-Dubreuil, Louis, *Le Raid Citroën. La première Traversée du Sahara en automobile, de Touggourt à Tombouctou par l'Atlantique* (The Black Journey. Across Central Africa with the Citroën expedition) (Paris: Plon, 1924; London: Geoffrey Bles. 1928).

Leiris, Michel, *L'Afrique fantôme* (Paris: Gallimard, 1934, also "Tel" Collection).

Londres, Albert, *Terre d'ébène* (Paris: Albin Michel, 1929 also "Arléa-poche" Collection).

Watteville, Vivienne de, *Speak to the Earth* (London: Methuen, 1935).

### Books about explorers and journeys of exploration

Arnaut, Robert, *Sur les traces de Stanley et de Brazza* (Paris: Mercure de France, 1989).

Broc, *Numa, Dictionnaire illustré des explorateurs français du xixe siècle (Afrique)* (Paris: Editions du Comité des travaux historiques et scientifiques, 1988).

Chevallier, Auguste, *Michel Adanson, voyageur, naturaliste et philosophe*, "Médaillons coloniaux" Collection (Paris: Larose, 1934).

Deschamps, Hubert, *Histoire des explorations*, "Que sais-je ?" Collection (Paris: PUF, 1969).

Hugon, Anne, *L'Afrique des explorateurs* (The Exploration of Africa from Cairo to the Cape), "Découvertes" Collection (Paris: Gallimard, 1991; London: Thames & Hudson, 1993).

_, *Vers Tombouctou*, "Découvertes"Collection (Paris: Gallimard, 1994).

Quella-Villéger, Alain, *René Caillié, une vie pour Tombouctou* (Poitier: Atlantique, 1999).

Ricard, Alain, *Voyages de découvertes en Afrique*, (anthology, with biographical details of explorers), "Bouquins" Collection (Paris: Robert Laffont, 2000).

### General reference

Comte, Gilbert, *L'Empire triomphant, 1871-1936* (Paris: Denoël, 1988).

Cornevin, Robert (collected work directed by) *Hommes et destins. Dictionnaire biographique d'outre-mer* (Paris: Académie des sciences d'outre-mer, 1975).

Dapper, Olfert, *Description of Benin* (Madison, Wisconsin: University of Wisconsin Press, August 1998).

Deschamps, Hubert (collective work directed by), *Histoire générale de l'Afrique noire*, 2 vols. (Paris: PUF, 1971).

Ki-Zerbo, Joseph, *Histoire de l'Afrique noire* (Paris: Hatier, 1972).

Lugan, Bernard, *Atlas historique de l'Afrique des origines à nos jours* (Paris: Editions du Rocher, 2001).

Mauny, Raymond, *Les Siècles obscurs de l'Afrique noire* (Paris: Fayard, 1970).

Péroncel-Hugoz, Jean-Pierre, *Le Fils rouge portugais* (Paris: Bartillat, 2002).

Wesseling, Henri, *Verdeel en Heers de deling van Afrika, 1880-1914* (Divide and rule. the partition of Africa, 1880-1914) (Amsterdam: Bert Bakker, 1992; London: Praeger, 1996).

### Monographs

Bergougniou, Jean-Michel, Clignet, Rémi, and David, Philippe, *Villages Noirs en France et en Europe (1870-1940)* (Paris: Karthala, 2001).

Chastanet, Monique (directed by) *Plantes et paysages d'Afrique* (Paris: Karthala, 1998).

Hodeir, Catherine, and Pierre, Michel, *L'Exposition coloniale* (Brussels: Complexe 1991).

Laissus, Yves, et Petter, Jean-Jacques, *Les Animaux du Muséum* (Paris: Imprimerie nationale, 1993).

Laissus, Yves, *Le Muséum national d'histoire naturelle*, "Découvertes" Collection (Paris: Gallimard, 1995).

Lejeune, Dominique, *Les Sociétés de géographie en France et l'expansion coloniale au xixe siècle* (Paris: Albin Michel, 1993).

Renault, François and Daget, Serge, *Les Traites négrières en Afrique* (Paris: Karthala, 1985).

Sofowora, Abayomi, *Medicinal plants and traditional medicine in Africa* (Chichester, UK: Wiley, 1982).

Webster, Paul, *Fachoda, la bataille pour le Nil* (Paris: éditions du Félin, 2001).

# Illustrations and photographic credits

**Abbreviations:** *t: top; b: bottom; l: left; r : right ; m: middle*

p. 4: © Bianchetti/Leemage.
p. 6: Cabinet des estampes, Bibliothèque Nationale, Paris © Photothèque Hachette.
p. 8: Musée du Louvre, Paris © RMN-Hervé Lewandowski.
p. 9 h: *In Monuments de l'Égypte et de la Nubie*, Bibliothèque Nationale, Paris © Bridgeman/Archives Charmet.
p. 9 b: Glyptothek, Munich © AKG.
p. 10-11: National Museum of Archaeology, Naples © G. dagli Orti.
p. 13: Bristol City Museum and Art Gallery © Bridgeman Art Library.
p. 14: Museu Nacional de Arte Antiga, Lisbon © Artephot/H. Stierlin.
p. 15 g: in *Livre des Armadas*, Lisbon Academy of Science, Lisbon © Photothèque Hachette.
p. 15 r: British Library, London © Bridgeman Art Library.
p. 16 From l to r and b to t: Cabinet from estampes, Bibliothèque Nationale, Paris © Photothèque Hachette.
p. 17 t: © AKG.
p. 17 m: British Museum, London © Photothèque Hachette.
p. 18: British Museum, London © AKG.
p. 19 l: British Museum, London © Bridgeman Art Library.
p. 19 r: Victoria & Albert Museum, London © Bridgeman Art Library.
p. 20 b: Société de géographie, Bibliothèque Nationale, Paris © Photothèque Hachette.
p. 20 t: British Museum, London © Bridgeman Art Library.
p. 21: Bibliothèque Nationale, Paris © Bridgeman/Archives Charmet.
p. 22 t: Château de Versailles © RMN-Franck Raux.
p. 22 b: In Plantes de la Martinique et de la Guadeloupe, 1688, Bibliothèque Nationale, Paris © AKG.
p. 23: The Natural History Museum Botany Library, London © Bridgeman Art Library.
p. 24 and 25: Engravings from Buffon's collection of quadruped animals, consisting of 362 color plates arranged by order and genus according to the Linné system of animal classification, Cabinet des estampes, Bibliothèque Nationale, Paris © Photothèque Hachette.
p. 26: Musée des Arts d'Afrique et d'Océanie, Paris © Bridgeman/Archives Charmet.
p. 27 t: In Le Tour du monde © Photothèque Hachette.
p. 27 b: Bareiss Collection © AKG.
p. 28: Plate from *Voyages de M. le Vaillant dans l'intérieur de l'Afrique par le Cap de Bonne-Espérance 1780-1785*, Bibliothèque Nationale, Paris © Bridgeman/Archives Charmet.
p. 29: Plate from *Voyage aux Indes orientales et en Chine*, Bibliothèque Nationale, Paris © Photothèque Hachette.
p. 30: Chartes and maps, Bibliothèque Nationale, Paris © Photothèque Hachette
p. 31 t: Musée des Arts d'Afrique et d'Océanie , Paris © RMN-J. G. Berizzi.
p. 31 b: Plate from *Voyage en Afrique de Vaillant, 1795*, Bibliothèque Marciana, Venise © G. dagli Orti.
p. 32: Musée de la Marine, Paris © Roger Viollet.
p. 33: Musée des Arts d'Afrique et d'Océanie, Paris © G. dagli Orti.
p. 35: Bibliothèque des Arts Décoratifs, Paris © Bridgeman/Archives Charmet.
p. 36 t: Musée des Arts d'Afrique et d'Océanie, Paris © G. dagli Orti.
p. 36 b: © AKG.
p. 37 l: Bibliothèque Nationale, Paris © Photothèque Hachette.
p. 37 r: © Photothèque Hachette.
p. 38-39: Cabinet des estampes, Bibliothèque Nationale, Paris © Photothèque Hachette.
p. 40: Musée du Louvre © RMN-Arnaudet.
p. 43: In *Le Tour du monde*, 1880 (2e semestre) © Photothèque Hachette.
p. 44: Musée des Arts d'Afrique et d'Océanie, Paris © G. dagli Orti.
p. 45 t: In *Voyage dans le Soudan occidental par Eugène Mage*, Hachette 1868 © Photothèque Hachette.
p. 45 b: © AKG.
p. 46-47: © Jean-Luc Manaud/Rapho.
p. 49: Musée des Arts d'Afrique et d'Océanie, Paris © G. dagli Orti.
p. 50: © AKG.
p. 51: Royal Geographical Society, London © Bridgeman Art Library.
p. 52 l: © Photothèque Hachette.
p. 52 r: in *Voyage autour du monde de la Favorite*, Arthus-Bertrand, Paris, 1835, Bibliothèque municipale, Versailles © Jean Vigne.
p. 53: Bibliothèque Nationale, Paris © Photothèque Hachette.
p. 54 t: Musée des Arts d'Afrique et d'Océanie, Paris © G. dagli Orti.
p. 54 m: in *Narrative of travels in Central Africa*, London, 1826, Bibliothèque du musée de l'Homme, Paris © Photothèque Hachette.
p. 55 l: © Bibliothèque Nationale de France .
p. 55 r: © Bibliothèque Nationale de France.
p. 56: in *Note de voyage à Tombouctou et à Jennes dans l'Afrique centrale, par René Caillié avec des remarques géographiques de Jomard*, Paris, 1830, Bibliothèque Nationale © Photothèque Hachette.
p. 57: © Selva/Leemage
p. 58: © Photothèque Hachette.
p. 59: Bib. Institut, Leipzig © AKG.
p. 60: in *Note de voyage à Tombouctou et à Jennes dans l'Afrique centrale, par René Caillié avec des remarques géographiques de Jomard*, Paris, 1830, Bibliothèque Nationale © Photothèque Hachette.
p. 61: Illustration by Riou from *Cinq semaines en ballon*, (Five Weeks in a Balloon) by Jules Verne © Photothèque Hachette.
p. 62: © AKG.
p. 63: British Library, London © Bridgeman Art Library.
p. 64 l: In *Le Tour du monde*, 1860 (2e semestre), Librairie Hachette © Photothèque Hachette.
p. 64 r: In *Le Tour du monde*, 1860 (2e semestre), Librairie Hachette © Photothèque Hachette.
p. 65: In *Voyage au Soudan et dans l'Afrique septentrionale, Bibliothèque des Arts décoratifs*, Paris © Bridgeman/Archives Charmet.
p. 66: In *Nouvel atlas de géographie par E. Cortambert*, Librairie Hachette, Paris © Photothèque Hachette.
p. 67: In *Le Petit Journal*, January 1894, Bibliothèque Nationale © Photothèque Hachette.
p. 68: Royal Geographical Society, London © Bridgeman Art Library.
p. 70: Private Collection © Bridgeman Art Library.
p. 71: © Hulton-Deutsch Collection/Corbis.
p. 72-73: © Christian Sappa/Rapho.
p. 74: In *Le Tour du monde*, 1864 (1er semestre), Librairie Hachette © Photothèque Hachette.
p. 75: © G. dagli Orti.
p. 76 t: © Rue des Archives.
p. 76 b: In *Le Tour du monde*, 1864 (1er semestre), Librairie Hachette © Photothèque Hachette.
p. 77 l and r: © Roger Viollet.
p. 78 and 79 t: Société de géographie, Paris © G. dagli Orti.
p. 79 b: Yann Arthus-Bertrand/Corbis.
p. 80-81:© Royal Geographical Society.
p. 82: © Abecasis/Leemage.
p. 83: In *Le Tour du monde*, 1864 (1er semestre), Librairie Hachette © Photothèque Hachette.
p. 84-85: Société de géographie, Paris © G. dagli Orti.
p. 86-87: Christie's Images, London © Bridgeman Art Library.
p. 88: Royal Geographical Society, London © Bridgeman Art Library.
p. 89: Musée des Arts d'Afrique et d'Océanie, Paris © G. dagli Orti.
p. 90 tr: © Rue des Archives/Granger Collection.
p. 90 tl and br: Royal Geographical Society, London © Bridgeman Art Library.
p. 90 b: British Library, London © Bridgeman Art Library.
p. 91: In *Voyage dans le sud-ouest de l'Afrique* (Explorations in South West Africa) by Thomas Baines, 1869, Librairie Hachette © Photothèque Hachette.
p. 92: In *Le Tour du monde, sous la dir. d'Édouard Charton*, 1873 (1er semestre), Librairie Hachette © Photothèque Hachette.
p. 93 t: © Selva/Leemage.
p. 93 b: In *Le Tour du monde, sous la dir. d'Édouard Charton*, 1873 (1er semestre), Librairie Hachette © Photothèque Hachette.
p. 94-95: Private Collection © Bridgeman Art Library.
p. 95 b: In *Le Tour du monde, sous la dir. d'Édouard Charton*, 1875 (2e semestre), Librairie Hachette © Photothèque Hachette.
p. 96: Gallery of Hungarian art, Budàpest © G. dagli Orti.
p. 97: © G. Sioen/Rapho.
p. 98: © Bridgeman Art Gallery/Michael Graham-Stewart.
p. 100: In *Au cœur de l'Afrique 1868-1871* (The Heart of Africa), vol. 1, 1875, Librairie Hachette, Paris © Photothèque Hachette.
p. 101: © Bridgeman/The Stapleton Collection.
p. 102-103: © Pascal Maitre/Cosmos.
p. 104 t: In *Au cœur de l'Afrique 1868-1871* (The Heart of Africa), vol.1,1875, Librairie Hachette, Paris © Photothèque Hachette.
p. 104 b: Bibliothèque Mazarine, Paris © Bridgeman/Archives Charmet.

p. 105: © Roger Viollet.
p. 106: In *Au cœur de l'Afrique 1868-1871* (The Heart of Africa), vol.1,1875, Librairie Hachette, Paris © Photothèque Hachette.
p. 107t and b: In *Au cœur de l'Afrique 1868-1871* (The Heart of Africa), vol.1,1875, Librairie Hachette, Paris © Photothèque Hachette.
p. 107 m: In *Au cœur de l'Afrique 1868-1871* (The Heart of Africa), vol.2,1875,Librairie Hachette, Paris © Photothèque Hachette.
p. 108: In *Le Tour du monde, sous la dir. d'Édouard Charton*, 1878 (2e semestre), Librairie Hachette © Photothèque Hachette.
p. 109 t: © Bridgeman/Giraudon-Lauros.
p. 109 b: © Selva/Leemage.
p. 110 tl: In *A travers le continent mystérieux* (Through the Dark Continent), Henry M. Stanley, vol. 2, 1879, Librairie Hachette © Photothèque Hachette.
p. 110 tr: In *Le Tour du monde, sous la dir. d'Édouard Charton*, 1878 (2e semestre), Librairie Hachette © Photothèque Hachette.
p. 110 m: In *Le Tour du monde, sous la dir. d'Édouard Charton*, 1878 (2e semestre), Librairie Hachette © Photothèque Hachette.
p. 110 bl and br: In *Le Tour du monde, sous la dir. d'Édouard Charton*, 1878 (2e semestre), Librairie Hachette © Photothèque Hachette.
p. 111 tl: In *Le Tour du monde, sous la dir. d'Édouard Charton*, 1878 (2e semestre), Librairie Hachette © Photothèque Hachette.
p. 111 tr: In *Le Tour du monde, sous la dir. d'Édouard Charton*, 1878 (2e semestre), Librairie Hachette © Photothèque Hachette.
p. 111b: In *Le Tour du monde, sous la dir. d'Édouard Charton*, 1878 (2e semestre), Librairie Hachette © Photothèque Hachette.
p. 112 t: In *Le Petit Journal*, mars 1905 © G. dagli Orti.
p. 112 b: © Bridgeman/Archives Charmet.
p. 113: Bibliothèque Nationale, Paris © Bridgeman/Giraudon-Lauros.
p. 114-115: © Pascal Maitre/Cosmos.
p. 116: In *Le Tour du monde, sous la dir. d'Édouard Charton*, 1878 (2e semestre), Librairie Hachette © Photothèque Hachette.
p. 117: © Roger Viollet.
p. 118: © Photothèque Hachette/Vérascope Richard.
p. 119: In *Le Tour du monde, sous la dir. d'Édouard Charton*, 1878 (2e semestre), Librairie Hachette © Photothèque Hachette.
p. 120 b: © AKG.
p. 120 t: Royal Geographical Society © Bridgeman Art Library.
p. 121: Département des Imprimés, Bibliothèque Nationale, Paris © Photothèque Hachette.
p. 122 and 123: In *Le Tour du monde, sous la dir. d'Édouard Charton*, 1878 (2e semestre), Librairie Hachette © Photothèque Hachette.
p. 124-125: © Bridgeman/Archives Charmet.
p. 126 t and b: In *A travers le continent mystérieux* (Through the Dark Continent), Henry M. Stanley, vol. 2, 1879, Librairie Hachette © Photothèque Hachette.
p. 127: In *Sahara et Soudan*, vol. 1,1881, Librairie Hachette, Paris © Photothèque Hachette.
p. 128: Private collection © Bridgeman Art Library.
p. 128-129: Bibliothèque des Arts décoratifs, Paris © Bridgeman/Archives Charmet.
p. 130: © AKG.
p. 131: In *Au cœur de l'Afrique 1868-1871* (The Heart of Africa) vol. 2, 1875, Librairie Hachette, Paris © Photothèque Hachette.
p. 132: Royal Geographical Society © Bridgeman Art Library.
p. 133: © AKG.
p. 134: Musée des Arts d'Afrique et d'Océanie © RMN.
p. 136 m: Musée des Arts d'Afrique et d'Océanie © RMN.
p. 136 t: © Leemage.
p. 137: © Roger Viollet.
p. 138-139: © Picture Library, National Portrait Gallery, London.
p. 140 t and m: In *Voyage au Soudan français (Haut Niger et Pays de Ségou) 1879-1881, par le commandant Galliéni*, 1885, Librairie Hachette © Photothèque Hachette.
p. 141 t: © Roger Viollet.
p. 141 b: Musée de Versailles et du Trianon © RMN/Arnaudet/G. B.
p. 142 t: © Roger Viollet.
p. 142 b: In *Voyage au Soudan français (Haut Niger et Pays de Ségou) 1879-1881, par le commandant Galliéni*, 1885, Librairie Hachette © Photothèque Hachette.
p. 143: © Roger Viollet.
p. 144 t: Royal Geographical Society, London © Bridgeman Art Library.
p. 144 b: In *Journal des voyages et des aventures de terre et de mer*, September1882 © Roger Viollet.

p. 145: Cabinet des Estampes, Bibliothèque Nationale, Paris © Photothèque Hachette.
p. 146 t and m: © AKG.
p. 147: © Bridgeman Art Library/Michael Graham-Stewart.
p. 148-149: In *Voyage pittoresque à travers l'Isthme de Suez de Marius Fontane*, Bibliothèque des Arts Décoratifs, Paris, © Bridgeman Art Library.
p. 150: © Costa/Leemage.
p. 151, 152, 153: © Roger Viollet.
p. 154: © AKG.
p. 155: Leeds Museums and Galleries (City Art Gallery) © Bridgeman Art Library.
p. 156: Musée de Versailles et du Trianon © RMN/Arnaudet.
p. 157: © Selva/Leemage.
p. 158: © G. dagli Orti.
p. 159 and 160: In *Du Niger au Golfe de Guinée (par le pays de Kong et le Mossi) par le capitaine Binger*, vol. 1, 1892, Librairie Hachette © Photothèque Hachette.
p. 161: © Bianchetti/Leemage.
p. 162 t: In *Le Journal illustré*, October 1892 © Roger Viollet.
p. 162 b: In *Le Petit Journal*, 1894, Bibliothèque Nationale, Paris © Photothèque Hachette
p. 163: Musée des Arts d'Afrique et d'Océanie © RMN/P. Bernard.
p. 164: Museum of Mankind, London © Bridgeman Art Library.
p. 165: In *À travers l'Afrique Centrale. Du Congo au Niger. 1892-1893 par Camille Maistre*, 1895, Librairie Hachette © Photothèque Hachette.
p. 166 t, 170 m and 171: © Roger Viollet.
p. 168: Association française des collectionneurs de titres © Jean Vigne.
p. 169: Musée des Arts d'Afrique et d'Océanie © RMN/J. G. Berizzi.
p. 170: Musée des Arts d'Afrique et d'Océanie © RMN/C. Jean.
p. 172 m and 173: © BHVP, Patrick Leger.
p. 172 t: © AKG.
p.174-175: Gemäldegalerie. Dresde © AKG.
p. 176: © Rue des Archives.
p. 177: © Jean Vigne.
p. 179: in *Le Petit Journal*, November 1913 © G. dagli Orti.
p. 180: © AKG.
p.181 t: In *Explorations dans l'intérieur de l'Afrique australe* (Missionary Travels and Researches in South Africa), David Livingstone, 1859, Librairie Hachette © Photothèque Hachette.
p. 181 m: © Jean Vigne.
p. 182 and183: © Rue des Archives.
p. 184 l and 185: Musée des Arts d'Afrique et d'Océanie © RMN/J. G. Berizzi.
p. 184 r: Musée des Arts d'Afrique et d'Océanie, fond Haardt © RMN/J. G. Berizzi.
p. 187: National Gallery of Victoria, Melbourne © Bridgeman Art Library; © Man Ray Trust/Adagp, Paris 2002.
p. 188-189: © Jean-Luc Manaud/Rapho.
p. 190: © Collection musée de l'Homme, Paris, cliché Marcel Griaule.
p. 191: © Collection musée de l'Homme, Paris.
p.192: © Keystone.
p. 193: © Photothèque Hachette/Vérascope Richard.
p. 194-195: Musée des Arts d'Afrique et d'Océanie © RMN/Hervé Lewandowski.
p. 196 and 197: © Collection Kharbine Tapabor.
p. 198-199: © Collection Kharbine Tapabor.
p. 200: Bibliothèque Municipale, Versailles © Jean Vigne.
p. 201: © Jean Vigne.
p. 202-203: © Royal Geographical Society, London.
p. 204 l: © Photothèque Hachette/Vérascope Richard.
p. 204 r: Bibliothèque Municipale, Versailles © Jean Vigne.
p. 205: © Yann Arthus-Bertrand/Corbis.
p. 206: © Keystone.
p. 207: © Keystone.
p. 208-209: © Musée de l'Homme collection, Paris, photo by Marcel Griaule.

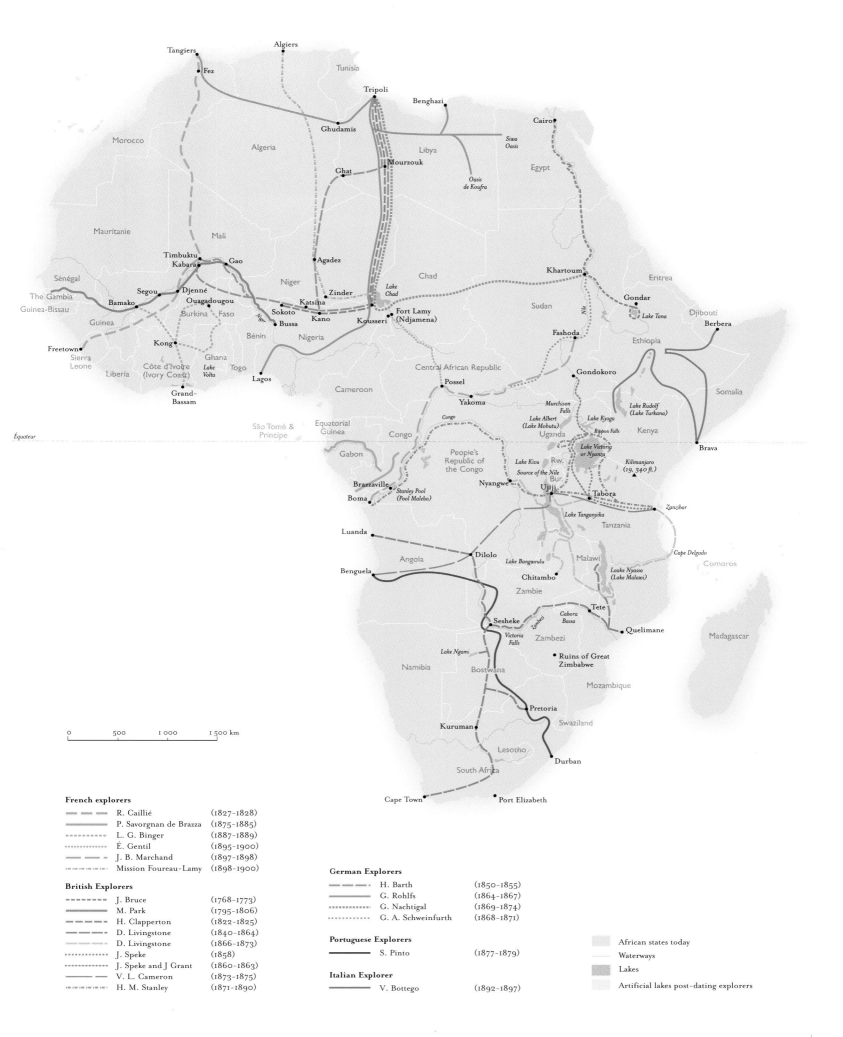

# Map of principal explorations

Tangiers • • Fez
Algiers •
Tunisia
Tripoli •
Benghazi •
Cairo •
Morocco
Algeria
Ghudamis •
Libya
*Siwa Oasis*
Egypt
Mourzouk •
Ghat •
*Oasis de Koufra*
Mauritanie
Mali
Agadez •
Chad
Khartoum •
Eritrea
Timbuktu • • Gao
Kabara •
Niger
Zinder •
*Lake Chad*
Gondar •
*Lake Tana*
Djibouti
Sénégal
Segou • Djenné
Ouagadougou
Katsina •
Sudan
*Nile*
Berbera •
The Gambia
Bamako •
Sokoto •
Kano •
Fort Lamy (Ndjamena) •
Fashoda •
Guinea-Bissau
Burkina Faso
Bussa •
Kousseri •
Ethiopia
Guinea
Kong •
Nigeria
Freetown •
Sierra Leone
Côte d'Ivoire (Ivory Coast)
Ghana
*Lake Volta*
Togo
Bénin
Lagos •
Somalia
Liberia
Grand-Bassam •
Cameroon
Central African Republic
Possel •
Gondokoro •
*Équateur*
São Tomé & Principe
Equatorial Guinea
Congo
Yakoma •
*Murchison Falls*
*Lake Albert (Lake Mobutu)*
*Lake Kyoga*
*Lake Rudolf (Lake Turkana)*
*Congo*
Uganda
*Ripon Falls*
Kenya
Gabon
People's Republic of the Congo
*Lake Kivu*
*Lake Victoria or Nyanza*
*Kilimanjaro (19,340 ft.)*
Brava •
Rw.
*Source of the Nile*
Bur.
Brazzaville •
Nyangwe •
Ujiji •
Tabora •
Boma •
*Stanley Pool (Pool Maleba)*
*Zanzibar*
Luanda •
*Lake Tanganyika*
Tanzania
*Cape Delgado*
Comoros
Dilolo •
*Lake Bangweulu*
Malawi
Angola
Benguela •
Chitambo •
*Laake Nyasa (Lake Malawi)*
Madagascar
Zambie
Tete •
Sesheke •
Cabora Bassa
Quelimane •
*Zambezi*
*Victoria Falls*
Zambezi
*Lake Ngami*
Ruins of Great Zimbabwe
Namibia
Bostwana
Mozambique
Pretoria •
Kuruman •
Swaziland
Cape Town •
Lesotho
Durban •
South Africa
Port Elizabeth •

| 0 | 500 | 1 000 | 1 500 km |

**French explorers**
— — — R. Caillié (1827-1828)
——— P. Savorgnan de Brazza (1875-1885)
·········· L. G. Binger (1887-1889)
·········· É. Gentil (1895-1900)
— — — J. B. Marchand (1897-1898)
—··—··— Mission Foureau-Lamy (1898-1900)

**British Explorers**
········· J. Bruce (1768-1773)
——— M. Park (1795-1806)
— — — H. Clapperton (1822-1825)
— — — D. Livingstone (1840-1864)
— — — D. Livingstone (1866-1873)
·········· J. Speke (1858)
·········· J. Speke and J Grant (1860-1863)
——— V. L. Cameron (1873-1875)
—··—··— H. M. Stanley (1871-1890)

**German Explorers**
— — — H. Barth (1850-1855)
——— G. Rohlfs (1864-1867)
·········· G. Nachtigal (1869-1874)
·········· G. A. Schweinfurth (1868-1871)

**Portuguese Explorers**
——— S. Pinto (1877-1879)

**Italian Explorer**
——— V. Bottego (1892-1897)

African states today
Waterways
Lakes
Artificial lakes post-dating explorers

**Editor:** Odile Perrard
**Creative Director:** Nancy Dorking
**Graphic design and production:** Emmanuel Barrault
**Cartography:** Cyril Suss - Hachette Tourisme
**Picture Research:** Véronique Brown and Anne Soto
**Editorial Secretary:** Stéphanie Mastronicola
**Proofreading:** Cécile Edrei

**Translated from the French by Florence Brutton**

This edition first published in the United States in 2003 by
The Overlook Press, Peter Mayer Publishers, Inc.
Woodstock, New York, and London

WOODSTOCK:
One Overlook Drive
Woodstock, NY 12498
www.overlookpress.com
[For individual orders, bulk and special sales, contact our Woodstock office]

NEW YORK:
141 Wooster Street
New York, NY 10012

LONDON:
Gerald Duckworth and Co. Ltd.
90-93 Cowcross Street
London EC1M 6BF
www.ducknet.co.uk

A CIP record for this book is available from the Library of Congress
Manufactured in Singapore
9 8 7 6 5 4 3 2 1
ISBN: 1-58567-498-2 (US)
ISBN: 0-7156-3292-2 (UK)

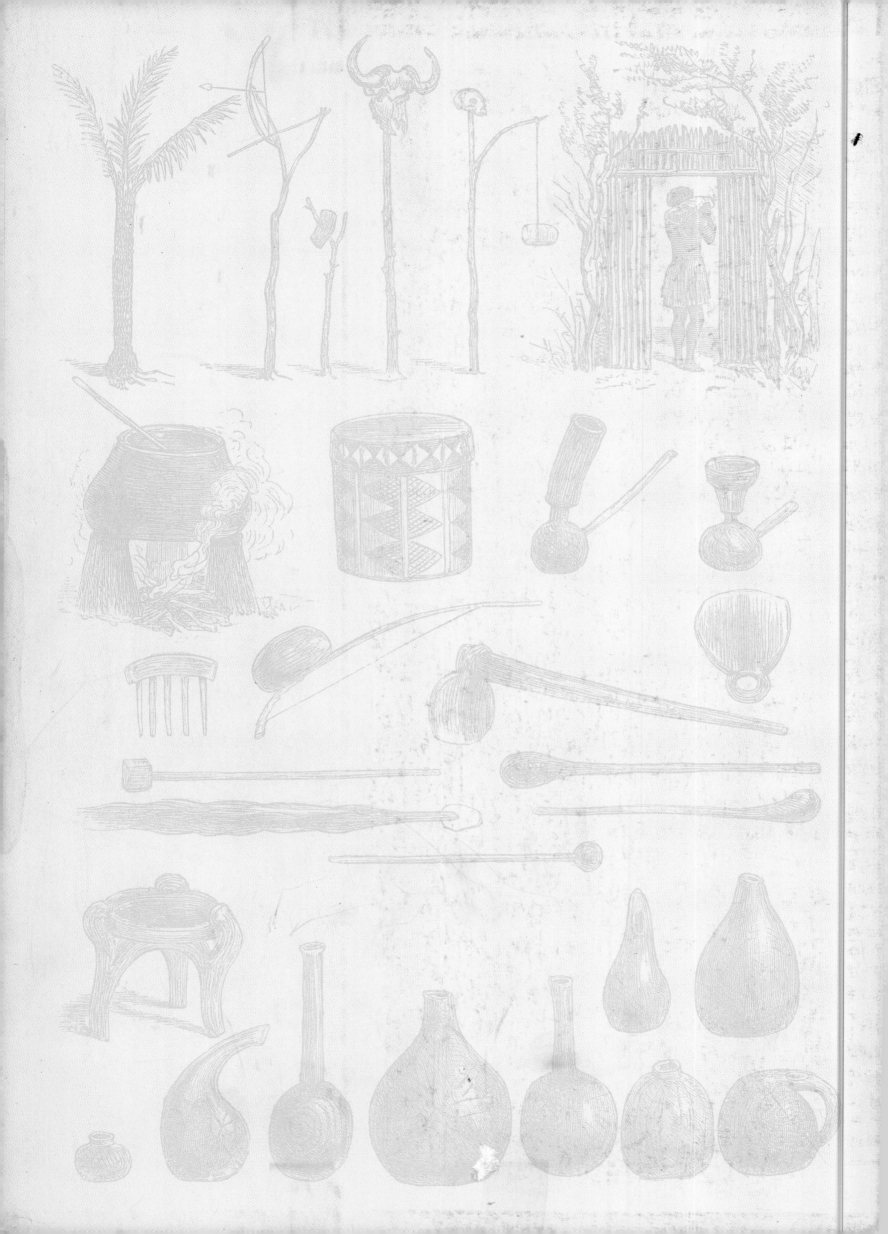